THUNDER *in the* MOUNTAINS

The men who built Ribblehead

WR MITCHELL

GREAT NORTHERN

THUNDER
in the
MOUNTAINS

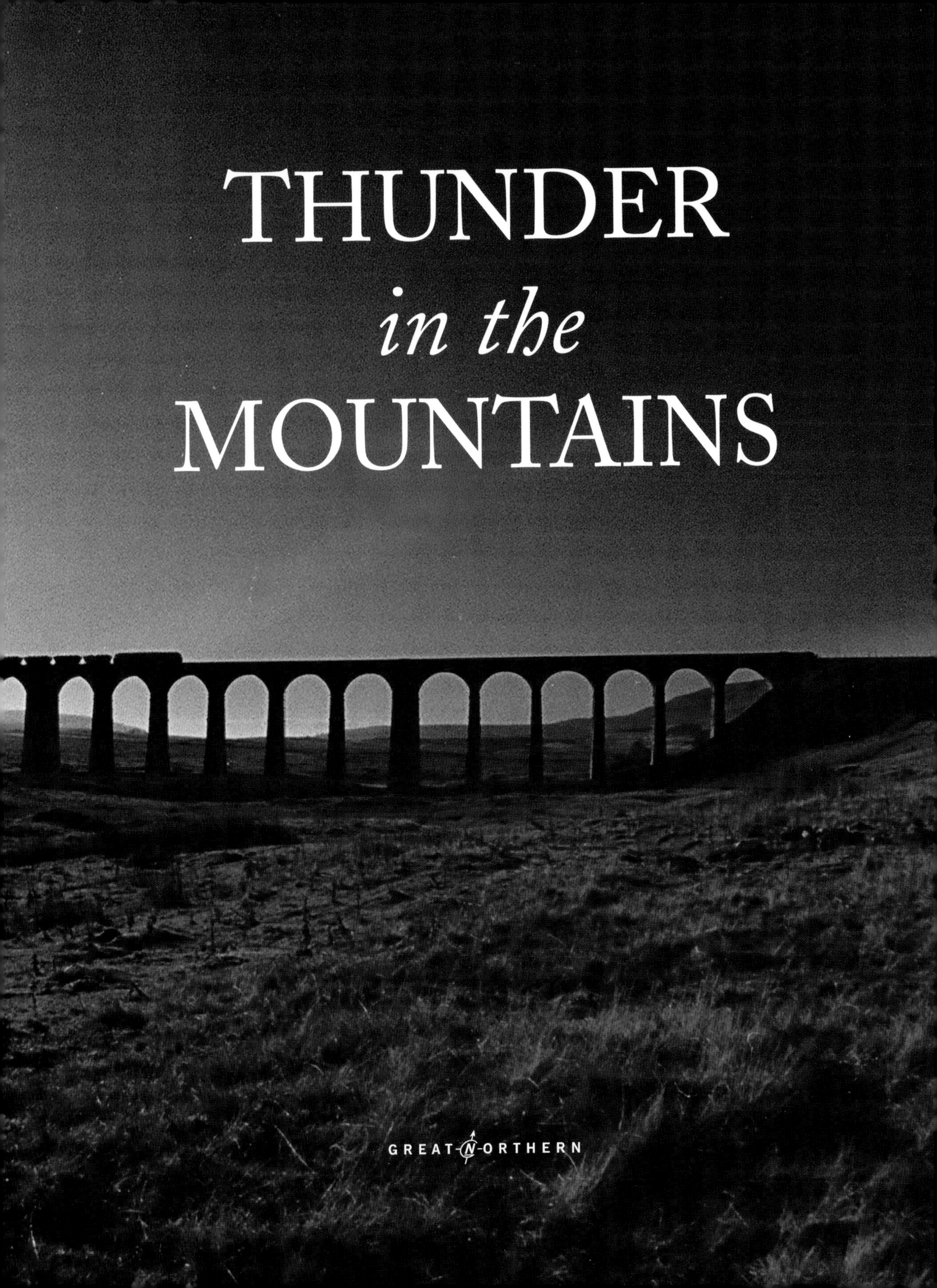

GREAT NORTHERN

Great Northern Books
PO Box 213, Ilkley, LS29 9WS
www.greatnorthernbooks.co.uk

ISBN: 978 1 905080 63 2

Design and layout: David Burrill

CIP Data
A catalogue for this book is available from the British Library

For an application form to join FoSCL
(The Friends of the Settle-Carlisle Line)
please send an sae to:
FoSCL Membership Secretary,
5 Dewhirst Road, Brighouse, W. Yorks HD6 4BA
or see the website www.settle-carlisle.co.uk

Contents

Ribblehead viaduct in summer sunlight with cloud-capped Whernside behind.

Introduction

My fascination with the Settle-Carlisle – a glorious culmination of the great age of railway building – began over 60 years ago. Having joined Harry J Scott at The Dalesman magazine I went out and about, on foot or bike, collecting material about people and places. I was drawn to Ribblehead by the sight of a harmonium in the corner of the station waiting room. At the viaduct I picked up a brick made of local clay mixed with shale. It was the type used under the viaduct's arches. A local man showed me the desk used on pay day for the men who built this spectacular stretch of line.

Harry Scott, with a Quaker background, put people before places. And so did I. My main interest in the Settle-Carlisle was not in technical matters but in human activity. Who built it? Who maintains it? Ribblehead viaduct, gloriously curved and set against a backdrop of Whernside, was especially interesting when I found the grave of the man who had supervised its construction. A walk across Blea Moor, and the sight of brick structures – the tops of ventilation shafts – looking like red pimples, on a moortop, became more significant when I chatted with a man who was lowered down one of them to clean out the drainage system.

Settle-Carlislitis, an incurable condition, was alleviated with the sight of steam-hauled trains on their 740-ft climb from Settle to Aisgill, a stretch known as the Long Drag. Ted Boak, my godfather, one of the Settle-Carlisle drivers, mentioned stormy days at Ribblehead viaduct when he and the fireman avoided the blast by sitting where it was sheltered until the short turbulent dash across the viaduct was over.

In this book, two major engineering feats – Ribblehead viaduct and Blea Moor tunnel – have been selected for special attention. Bearing in mind what Harry Scott had said about people before things, I have based this book on folk activity as well as engineering feats. I researched the little-known life of Job Hirst, who in the early 1870s supervised the early stages of the viaduct's construction. A life of fulfilment came to a premature end when, returning in a horse-drawn trap from Ingleton, he was attacked, robbed and within a short time had died.

Through a friendship with Tony Freschini, resident engineer during a modern restoration, I saw men on special scaffolding re-bricking under the arches, temporarily exposing some of the original bricks, formed of local clay and shale. Damaged blocks of limestone were deftly replaced by concrete, tinted to match the original stone, set in a mould that was afterwards sculptured to preserve naturalness and so that no two stones were alike.

I have, with permission, walked across the viaduct. In the 1960s I had the privilege of joining

Ribblehead from the air, with Princess Elizabeth crossing with an up express. Ingleborough looms in the background.

Diesel power on Ribblehead viaduct.

Stormy sky at Ribblehead station.

Blea Moor looking towards Ingleborough with a distant glimpse of the signal box.

The viaduct at the close of the year 1985. Whernside is well covered in snow.

an inspection party in Blea Moor. The "down" line was still in use. I stood at a depth of 500-ft below the moor top, in what a local signalman had called "The Toob", as a steam-hauled goods train thundered by a few yards away. A BR man suggested that I tuck my trouser legs into my socks. Otherwise smoke would pour from underneath my shirt!

The finest record of the construction period is to be found in the pages of the Lancaster Guardian which, like many another researcher, I have quarried extensively. The contemporary accounts have been updated by tape-recorded interviews with old-timers, long dead, but not forgotten. The story is given a richly human aspect through the memories of Harry Cox, Jack Towler and Nancy Edmondson, who in her young days lived in a cottage near the tracks. An account is given of a massed walk of over 2,000 people in 2007. It was permitted under strict controls by Network Rail and organised by the Friends of the Settle-Carlisle line.

The Settle-Carlisle, now often thought of by visitors as a heritage railway, has had its organisational ups and downs but remains a fast, all-weather main line, well-used today both by freight and passenger traffic. Many people suffer from Settle-Carlislitis. Bishop Eric Treacy, widely known for his passion for this form of transport, and his outstanding railway photography, ranked the Settle-Carlisle with two other north-country wonders, namely York Minster and Hadrian's Wall.

Chapter One

The Midland goes it alone – A contractor's caravan, living quarters for surveyors, arrives at Batty Green – Job Hirst, sub-contractor for a viaduct, samples the landscape and bitter weather – The sad story of Batty Wife Hole.

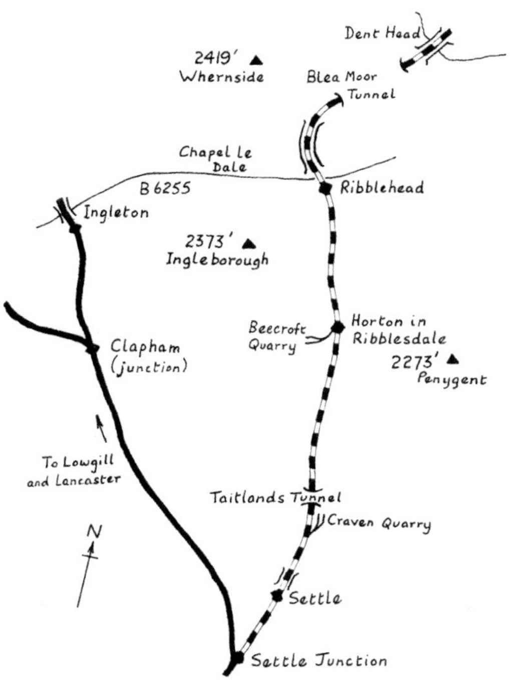

Sketch map of the southern portion of the Settle-Carlisle railway as far as Blea Moor tunnel. Also shown is the earlier Midland line to Ingleton.

In December, 1869, the cheerful tooting of a steam engine cut through frosty air in Chapel-le-Dale, a glacier-hewn valley near Ingleton, in north-west Yorkshire. Into view came a traction engine towing a caravan – the type of four-wheeled van favoured by travelling folk and roadmen. Its journey had begun in a contractor's yard in London. Its destination was a tract of moorland and peat-bog known as Batty Green. Here a group of surveyors and their assistants wintered, being employed on two major projects on the proposed Settle-Carlisle railway.

In its bid to reach Carlisle, gateway to Scotland, on its own metals, the Midland Railway used the north-south valleys, Ribble and Eden. In between lay a daunting terrain of fells and deep water-carved gills. A viaduct was planned where several valleys met at Batty Wife Hole. A tunnel would be driven through the heart of Blea Moor. Hundreds of men, scores of horses and whatever labour-saving equipment was available worked to a five-year target. Building the Settle-Carlisle Railway would take a little longer than this...

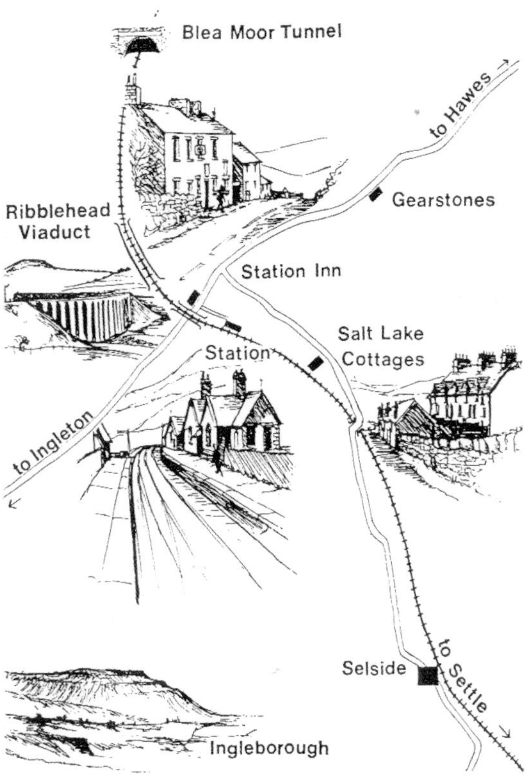

Features of the line between Selside and Blea Moor tunnel.

The caravan drew quizzical glances from a thin scattering of farm folk. As the surveyors moved around, with the heaviest equipment reposing on donkey-back, they put red grouse to whirring flight and startled the moorland sheep, which had stared with eyes as ancient-looking as the outcropping rock. The surveyors trod heather ground and peat-bog, where what appeared to be hard earth would, if disturbed, take on the consistency of Scotch broth.

Job Hirst, who had been charged with overseeing the construction of a large viaduct, was Yorkshire born and bred. He was devoting his working life to creating railway structures in stone. The Hirsts hailed from Kirkheaton, near Huddersfield. An improbable tale claimed the family had originated in Sherwood Forest, Nottingham and descended from Robin Hood! What Job knew for certain was that he was born in 1815, being the son of Joshua and Ellen Hirst.

A practical lad, on leaving school he became a mason and was taught the business of building "long bridges with spans". He was master mason on the Lockwood Viaduct, constructed between 1846 and 1848. He supervised the driving of a tunnel under part of Huddersfield, also working on "two stupendous viaducts crossing the valleys on the north and south sides of the town." Job impressed the Welsh by constructing a 17-span viaduct near Caerphilly. Its style was audacious – but it hadn't "tummelled" down!

Two views of the magnificent Lockwood viaduct, near Huddersfield, where Job Hirst cut his teeth as master mason between 1846 and 1848. He was only thirty-one when he took on the post.

Job courted and wed Mary Pickard, a Yorkshire lass who was ten years his junior. They were married at All Saints Church, Almondbury. She bore him four sons and a daughter. Walter, the apple of Job's eye, developed dad's flair for engineering. Job's career with stone, mortar and trowel took an upturn in 1856 when, in India, he constructed the viaducts and excavated the tunnels for the Bombay to Poona Railway. (The equipment he required when commissioned to do this work was lying in Brindisi, Italy. Job, who detested "faffing about", as he called doing nowt, promptly had it transferred to India.)

This wondrously hot, exotic land, had no labour problems, as in England. India teemed with men who were anxious to work. Job, in turn, impressed the Indians with his engineering skills. Yet after two years of hard labour, and with some major railway projects completed, he was back in Yorkshire with his family – and ready for another big railway job.

On being appointed to supervise the construction of a huge viaduct near the headwaters of the Ribble, Job entrained for Ingleton, which in Midland terms was the northernmost point of its large rail network. Clickety-click, clickety-click. As the train clattered from Bradford to the termination of the Midland system at Ingleton, on the Greta, there was time for Job to ponder on the rapid commercial rise of the Midland railway system.

It had begun when a group of businessmen organised the movement of coal by canal barge. They then latched on to the new passion for railways. With shrewd takeovers and profitable leases, they spread rail tracks over much of the country, ever-ready to expand as opportunities occurred.

Harsh conditions on Ingleborough, the majestic fell dominating the scene at Ribblehead.

The Settle-Carlisle project under discussion in Parliament.

They became strapped for cash. It did not dent their ambition to have a share in the lucrative Scottish trade.

Clickety-click, clickety-click. Job noticed during his train journey a change in the landscape – from gritstone to limestone. Now the skyline was crowned by Ingleborough, one of the big Pennine flat-tops. Thank god they didn't intend to drive a tunnel through that monster! Hedges had become walls made without a dab of mortar. Cows had become sheep – hundreds of sheep, close-cropping the ultra-green turf in the calm between rainy periods. Job had yet to experience the upland climate, as on Batty Green, where a tract of moorland, meeting place of several valleys, was doused by seventy inches of rain a year and beset by a wind that at times screamed like a banshee.

His thoughts returned to railway matters. The project sprang from inter-company rivalry (a not uncommon Victorian occurrence). The thrustful Midland Company ran into conflict with the London and North Western over the joint use of the Lancaster-Carlisle line and the Citadel station at Carlisle. So the Midland began to dream about a new route to Carlisle along which it could attract a greater share of the Anglo-Scottish traffic.

In 1865, in a second period of "railway mania", the North of England Railway, made up of Dales landowners, received Parliamentary approval for what was basically a line from Settle to Hawes, in Wensleydale. The Midland suggested a neat variant – a railway from Settle to Carlisle, with a branch to Hawes. It was approved. The London & North Western Railway tried for reconciliation. The Midland was keen to adopt it. The abandonment bill introduced to Parliament was rejected. The Midland must go it alone... Some people had their doubts that such a railway was possible. A morose farmer observed that between Settle and Carlisle there was not a level piece of ground large enough to build a house.

Alan Fearnley
75

Ribblehead viaduct under construction, from a painting by Alan Fearnley.

The first sod of the new line was cut at Anley, near Settle, in November, 1869. The line was planned as a first-class, high-speed, all-weather route, making use of two north-south valleys – Ribblesdale and the Eden Valley. Engineering solutions were found to problems arising in the tract of high fell-country in between the major dales.

The Hirst family – Job and his two sons, Charles and Walter – became associated with it when they met John Ashwell, who had won the No 1 Contract, ranging from Settle Junction to Denthead. Ashwell, of Kentish Town, North London, was a conscientious, hard-working type who had taken on a job he would not financially be able to sustain, especially as he had been persuaded by Crossley, the Engineer-in-Chief, to reduce his quoted figure.

What the railway-builders could not foresee was the weather at its Pennine worst. A fickle labour force. And the startling speed at which the project gobbled up money. As will be related, Ashwell gave up the contract and the Midland would complete the project by direct labour, with another Mr Ashwell (no relation) in local command.

In the closing stage of his rail journey to Ingleton, Job Hirst had two major imponderables about the viaduct in mind – the availability of skilled labour and sources of suitable stone. Building a railway was popularly thought of as a navvy-operation – virtually hand-made – but "steam travellers" operating on wooden framing would make light work of lifting stones of considerable size and weight, which could then be positioned on the piers. Hundreds of horses would work the wagons from which waste from excavations might be tipped for embankments.

Job Hirst had some experienced support. Ashwell, with the heaviest work on his patch, had appointed John de Lacy Duffy, an accomplished civil engineer as his manager, though he would be especially concerned with bridges at the southern end of the line. Duffy would have an unexpected problem, unrelated to engineering. His many Irish workers would be threatened by some of the English workers. He himself came under threat – of murder – when he told a miner at Batty Green that no beer was to be sold in the huts without a licence.

Job would also meet at Batty Green a bright young resident engineer named Edgar O. Ferguson and also a man known respectfully as Mr Davidson. He was an appointee of the Midland inspector, dealing with the stretch from "Ingleton Road to Dent Head Viaduct." As Job alighted from the train at Ingleton, he had major worries. He had been led to expect a workforce at the viaduct site of 60 or more masons and labourers. Would expectation be supported by fact?

Ingleton was a workaday village for many years. Old-time industries were coal-mining and quarrying. Now there was stirrings of railway life – a raw life, sustained by insistent bosses, craftsmen in stone and brick and gangs of tough, unfeeling labourers.

Men and materials for the new railway would be transported by horse and cart up Storrs Brow and through Chapel-le-Dale to Batty Green. On that first visit, in 1869, Job had a brief period of peace as he travelled through the U-shaped glacial valley lying between Ingleton and Batty Wife Hole, near the source of the Ribble, and hemmed in by Whernside and Ingleborough.

It was a calm between two storms. It was almost certain to rain on the morrow. The stormy aspect had been captured by Turner, the landscape painter, who in 1808, during a tour of the North, captured a stormy mood in water-colour: "Clouds swirl around the head of the mountain [Ingleborough]. A squally shower approaches. An alarmed figures makes for cover as lightning flashes through the dark clouds overhead."

The road that Job Hirst followed was little changed from its turnpike days but soon, in railway time, would have affinities with a ploughed field. Job saw thin sunlight seeping through mist. Naked limestone gleamed. There seemed to be as much outcropping rock as grass. Expanses of pearl-white limestone had been frost and rain-shattered into irregular blocks known as "clints". The cracks in between were known by another old dialect word – "grykes".

As a former stonemason, Job noticed how random pieces of limestone had been cleverly assembled into grey walls made without a dab of mortar. The courses were kept level even where they climbed the valley sides, enclosing rough grazings. Whernside and Ingleborough stared fixedly at each other across the dale.

Job, briefly visiting the little church, saw woodland that was so damp that rocks as well as trees were cocooned in moss. Not long after Turner's visit, the writer Robert Southey stayed at Weathercote House and included a verbal impression of the church in a strange little novel called The Doctor. Southey's lyrical impression reminds us of what it was like before the railway transformed local life – and filled the churchyard with men, women and (mainly) young children.

What did Southey see? He wrote: "The turf was as soft and fine as the adjoining hills; it was seldom broken, so scanty was the population to which it had appropriated...and the few tombstones which had been placed there were themselves half buried. The sheep came over the wall when they listed, and sometimes took shelter in the porch from the storm. Their voices and the cry of the kite wheeling above were the only sounds which were heard except when a single bell tinkled a service on the Sabbath day or a slower tongue gave notice that one of the children of the soil was returning to the earth from which he sprung."

For Job Hirst, his brief glimpse of the church was followed by a sojourn at the Hill Inn, an old hostelry which would be well patronised by navvies during the construction period. Mary Anne Lee was charged with dancing in an indecent manner with drunken navvies. In the future, with the Settle-Carlisle railway operating, the inn would be patronised by the well-to-do who were drawn to the area by its natural wonders.

The Hill Inn, an old hostelry on the route from Ingleton to Batty Green.

Called to the bar, Job Hurst sank a pint of ale – no more than a pint, for he had been brought up in West Riding Nonconformity. There followed a straight stretch of road that, had there been mist, would have been tedious, but today offered splendid views of the big hills on either side. At the head of Ribblesdale, Job's keen eyes located a drumlin-field, where material forsaken by long-melted glaciers, formed clustering low, rounded hills – the "basket of eggs" image used by less serious geologists.

The view had opened out. The road, now unfenced, crossed an area where several valleys met in a tract of heather and peat bogs. Job reflected that for the next few years this would be his home area. A breeze sprang up from nowhere – and stunted thorn trees began to wheeze like asthmatic old men. The area was pockmarked eerily by swallow-holes, natural shafts in the limestone. Batty Wife Hole, a celebrated pothole, soon to give its name to the largest of the hutment areas, was brimful of water.

Meeting up with the surveyors, at their dalehead caravan, Job heard the old tale of the demise of Batty's wife. She and her husband often quarrelled; they parted for the umpteenth time. Ere long, they were reconciled and would meet by the pothole. Mrs Batty, punctual as ever, was the first to return. He was not there. In a fit of despair, she threw herself into the pool and was drowned. Mr Batty, who had been delayed, and was now full of remorse, also drowned himself. A less serious version of the story was that the water-filled pothole – soon to be filled in more substantially – was used by Batty's wife and their children – on washday!

The surveyors who had arrived with the traction engine and caravan, now parked at the roadside, were wrapped in woollen clothes to cheat the wind. One of them told Job about the "lazy" winds – so lazy, indeed, they attempted to go through a man rather than taking the trouble to go round him. Donkeys had borne their heavy survey equipment to where the piers of the viaduct would be set. The surveyors felt sorry for the donkeys – critters that hailed from Mediterranean lands. Local farmers said their skins were not entirely water-and-chill proof. They kept their donkeys under cover in the worst of the weather.

William Towler, a native of Settle, was assisting the surveyors, holding their measuring tapes and associated equipment. One of the surveyors wryly observed that in 1751 a turnpike from Lancaster to Richmond, via Ribblehead, had been authorised by an Act of Parliament. Now, in 1869, Parliament had allowed an iron road to be constructed – a road heading towards a trackless north.

That night, a north-easterly gale delivered snow, clogging the vital approach road and altering the contours of the landscape the men were here to survey. As darkness came, one of the men stood by the van for half an hour, holding up a bull's-eye lantern as a guide to his fellows who were homecoming through the waste. If a man stuck in snow, his mates were handy to dig him out. More often, there was rain, followed by "two chain o' knee-deep water four times a day for the fellows atween their meat and their work." The surveyors who ascended Blea Moor to work out the position of tunnel shafts had tents.

Job found temporary lodgings at a farmhouse. The farmer railed about the decline of the old turnpike road from Ingleton. It was sadly overworked. In a wet spell, he said, "there'll be pools of water, loads of mire, deep and long cart ruts." Job was shown a critical parochial report from Ingleton asserting that "if the township shall neglect the mending of the roads until they have come to satisfactory terms with the railway contractors, there is no telling when the evil will be remedied."

Chapter Two

Young Sharland walks along the course the railway will take – John Ashwell, a Londoner, is awarded Contract No 1 – Job Hirst begins work on the viaduct – A mini-army of labourers arrives, some from the four corners of the land.

At first, a flurry of letters and forms. The Midland, bolstered by its Parliamentary Act, written in stilted phraseology, confirmed the company's legal access to specified "pieces or parcels of land". Each landowner received a copy of the document, also a plan with the specific claim marked in red. "And the Company hereby demand from you and every of you [sic] the particulars of your respective estates and interests in the premises so required, and of the claims made by you and every of you in respect thereof..."

Solicitors, with sheaves of documents, secured for the Midland the land that Parliament had granted. This was to be done amicably but firmly by arrangement with the owners. James Farrer, of Clapham, was a principal landowner, presiding over the Ingleborough estate, which extended over the hill to take in Blea Moor and Gearstones. It was primarily a sporting estate. In late summer, most of the landscape glowed purple as the bonnie heather bloomed and resounded to the crackle of gunfire.

Farrer, in making the land available to railway engineers, specified that on Blea Moor the telegraph wire to the signal box must be buried or it would become a hazard to the low-flying grouse. Job Hirst, a realist, smiled when told about a boggart said to inhabit Blea Moor. This supernatural being varied its boring life by hopping on and off horse-drawn vehicles on the nearby turnpike.

Mr Trethewy, the official law valuer for the Settle-Carlisle, asked the Construction Committee for a rise in the remuneration to be paid to him. He quoted "exceptional circumstances relating to the country of the proposed railway." He got a rise from £30 and £35 a mile. Trethewy found some difficulty in getting land under the 1867 Act. This led to a slowdown with regard to compulsory purchase.

The two top men were Sir James Joseph Allport, General Manager of the Midland, known – though not to his face – as the Bismark of Railway Politics, and John Sydney Crossley, Engineer-in-Chief for the Settle-Carlisle, who had a flying start to his railway career.

Crossley knew the area well. It was he who had arranged for a second line to be laid on the railway from Clapham junction to Ingleton, a vital depot during Settle-Carlisle days. Crossley designed the viaduct that Job Hirst would put in hand. And Crossley would report on the ups and downs of fortune during the construction period in monthly reports to the Construction Committee. He was a protégé of George Hudson, the nearest person the railway world had to a monarch.

John Crossley, chief engineer for the Settle-Carlisle line.

Allport and Crossley were not deskbound administrators. To familiarise themselves with the route, they strode along most of the proposed course. Crucial to the daring scheme of providing a middle-way to Scotland were two north-south valleys – Ribble and Eden. Those who surveyed the area, not least Allport, blanched at the sight of the north face of Blea Moor. A tunnel must be driven through this hill mass. The Moor so impressed Allport that when he retired from the railway he asked that an impression of Blea Moor and the northern portal of its tunnel should appear in the background to his portrait.

James Allport, general manager of the Midland Railway.

Allport had been disgruntled by the arrangements made between the Midland and the London & North Western, whose route to the Border was via Shap Fell. Said Allport: "It is a very rare thing for me to go down to Carlisle without being turned out twice. I have seen twelve or fifteen passengers turned out at Ingleton and the same number at Tebay...We have applied in vain for through carriages to Scotland over and over again...They will not book through from Glasgow to London through us...It is only recently that I had a correspondence with a family who particularly wanted to come by the Midland (from Glasgow to Derby), but they were refused and were sent by Crewe."

The official portrait of James Allport.

Charles Stanley Sharland, a Tasmanian, former assistant in the office of the Maryport and Carlisle Railway and a member of Crossley's staff, was invited to make the preliminary surveys. He walked every yard of the way, in winter, with a support party of six workmen. The party was snowed up at the isolated farm-cum-inn of Gearstones, near the source of the Ribble. A feat of tunnelling through snow led them to a water-trough in the yard. Gravely ill with tuberculosis, young Sharland withdrew from the project in November, 1870, at the age of 25 years; he died of tuberculosis at Torquay in the following March.

Charles Stanley Sharland, who surveyed the route of the Settle-Carlisle line but died before the project was completed.

The Settle-Carlisle was clearly no ordinary railway. The engineers could not afford to adopt a devil-may-care attitude to the rough and mountainous terrain. They made clever use of every topographical feature that barred their way. A Victorian engineer compared the profile of the line with a whale "lying on its belly, with its nose at Settle, its tail at Carlisle." This Settle-Carlisle whale would measure 22 miles from nose to crown of head, and a further 50 miles from here to the tip of the tail.

A surveying party determines the precise route of the line.

The surveyors worked in winter. At Ribblehead, the brief summer flush was like a wink between two long winters and no time must be lost. A Wesleyan local preacher, on a summertime preaching jaunt to Blea Moor, saw the district at its bountiful best. On the way to his appointment, the preacher had seen aspects of "nature's picture gallery...Hill and dale, heath and meadows, all looked charming..."

An initial welter of tenders, both original and revised, were dealt with by a Settle and Carlisle Construction Committee. On August 2, 1869, the tenders related to Contract No 1, from Settle to Denthead. Fourteen firms responded. The contract was secured by John Ashwell who, when his figure of £349,226 compared unfavourably with Crossley's estimate of £336,523, promptly revised it downwards. (For Ashwell, it was to prove a big mistake. Ashwell's funds would dry up long before completion and he would be forced to go, cap in hand, to the Midland for extra cash, leading him to forfeit the contract, which would be taken over by the railway company.)

The upper reaches of Littledale, from which blocks of limestone for the viaduct would be taken. Ingleborough is in the background.

At Batty Wife Hole, negotiations over land for the viaduct and for the right to burrow through Blea Moor were made with the agent of James Farrer, who in 1866, with other landowners, had opposed the Settle-Carlisle Bill. Farrer subsequently realised that in cash terms a railway was a good thing. Money would be received for the poor quality land on which the main viaduct would be built. Rent would be derived from the contractor for his works and the sites of the huts built for the workers. There would be royalties for stone quarried and for clay removed from below a peat bog in the process of brickmaking.

The prospect of a viaduct on the grand scale fired the imagination of railwaymen. Originally, the viaduct was named after its location – Batty Moss. A "moss" in the Pennine context is swampy ground colonised by sphagnum, a great peat-forming plant on the Pennines. The Victorian railway-builders encountered banks of peat up to nine feet thick. The dry ridges were covered by peat and when the first surveyors ranged across the area the crowing of red grouse – kowa, kowa – was heard on every hand.

Contract No 1, which was largely a highland area, was affected almost from the beginning by a shortage of labour and grim weather. The Construction Committee, meeting on 5 July, 1870, heard John Crossley's assessments of the situation. Crossley had postponed his retirement in order to supervise the construction of the Settle-Carlisle line. He reported in March that the number of men employed was 297. Work on Blea Moor tunnel, begun five months before, was in a backward state and very little exertion was visible.

A further report indicated that earth shifting was proceeding at about a third to two-fifths of the amount required for "on time" completion. Then things bucked up, as they say. By the end of July, Mr Ashwell was employing 1,489 men. The figure was to rise to 2,208, then fall to 1,453. Bad weather curtailed work at the northern end of the contract. Some cuttings were inaccessible, presumably through a heavy snowfall. "The rate [of work] is about half the required average."

January 3 – and the same sorry tale was related by Crossley in his report to the Construction Committee. Contracts 1, 2 and 3 were being slowed down by very severe weather. On Ashwell's contract, many cuttings were blocked. The workforce was down to little over half the summer figure. A year later, Ashwell, in financial trouble, was applying for loans – and getting them from an increasingly desperate railway company.

In May 1871, Crossley and a colleague named Hodges were requested to visit Settle and investigate the affairs of the contractor. Mr Ashwell's books and the works on Contract No 1 were examined. The cost of the separate parts of the contract were compared with the amounts paid by the company for them. The conclusion? "We are of the opinion that there is a reasonable expectation of the contract being completed with risk of loss if proper superintendence and care have been exercised." Perhaps.

Meanwhile, work was proceeding on what would be the showpiece of Contract No 1 – the viaduct across Batty Green. The first stone had been laid on October 12, 1870. The work was under the superintendence of Job Hirst. His concerns included the well-being of around 60 masons, the availability of sufficient Barrow lime, brought in from the neighbourhood of Leicester, and the reliability of a 10 h.p. engine, constantly employed for mixing mortar. Job Hirst studied the degree of hardness of the quarried stone in Littledale. He was concerned at the proneness of a "mountain stream", flushed by heavy rainfall, to flood the two areas in which quarrying was taking place. A steam pump was to be installed to improve the drainage.

According to Job's foreman, it would be two years at the early rate of progress before the viaduct would be completed. And with foundations laid 25-ft below ground, a casual visitor to the site could not appreciate the true extent of the progress made. Edward Shipley Ellis, deputy chairman, later chairman of the Midland, had the unenviable task of reporting to the shareholders details of how the railway was progressing. He acquired his information at first-hand.

In September, 1871, Crossley reported the unhappy news of the demise of Mr Ashwell's contract with the company. Reasonable terms had been negotiated. "The management of Contract No 1 has been entirely in the company's direction from the middle of September when it will be seen in the next few months whether any improvement will have occurred."

Ashwell, who had borrowed no less than £50,000 and still failed, had surrendered his contract to the company. He was paid £10,000 in discharge.

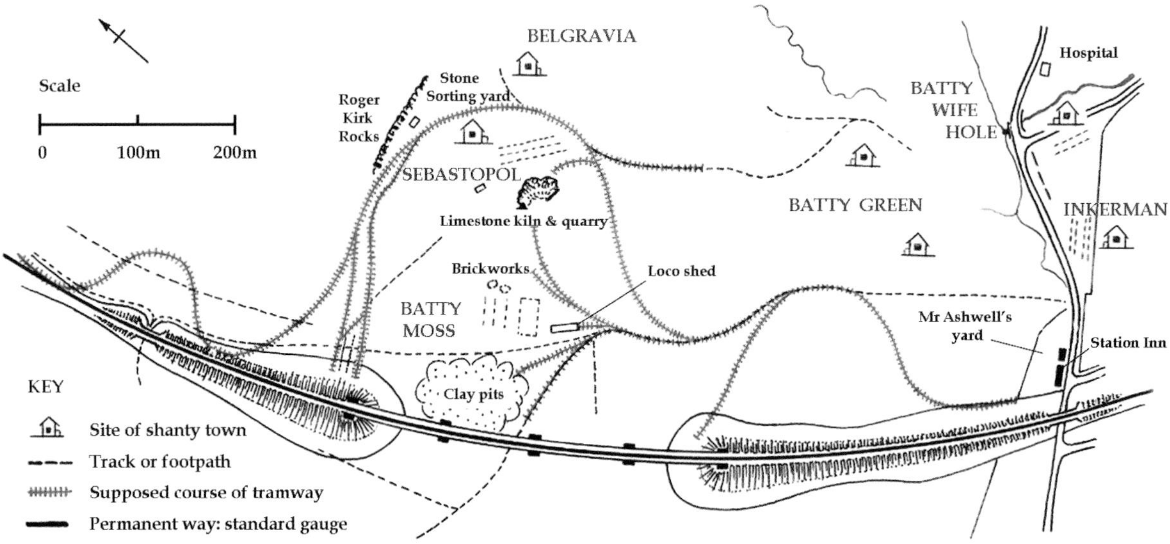

Shanty towns and contractors' tramways at Ribblehead.

Masons trimming blocks of limestone to size for use on the viaduct.

Chapter Three

Men and equipment are mustered – Batty Moss is transformed – The viaduct (Bridge 66) takes shape – And miners begin driving a tunnel through a lonely moor - A locomotive is delivered: by road.

Job Hirst, sub-contractor on Batty Moss viaduct, had a modest lodging for his family – No 2 Batty Wife Hole. Despite its earthy name, it was in a salubrious area, beside the turnpike road, well clear of the boggy area. Job was head of a family that included his wife Mary, sons Charles, Walter and Joshua and a daughter called Nancy. There was no rent, no rates.

His workplace, the viaduct, was plainly visible when he stood at the door of the hut; it was an easy walk away from where he ate and slept. The road to Ingleton had degenerated through excessive use. Job heard that when fuel was needed for the brickworks and to keep the home fires burning, an estimated 600 tons of coal per month would be needed on Contract No 1 alone.

In railway building, the largest and most difficult projects were tackled first. The viaduct came into this category. It was in 1870 that the ground was disturbed for the first few foundations of piers that would eventually seem to block out half the sky. The area to the west of the proposed viaduct would retain its moorland state, pockmarked by swallow holes. On this Ingleton side of the viaduct lay the worst mosses – Gunner Fleet Moss and Low Moss, Parker's Moss and Bruntscar Moss.

The tract of moorland known as Batty Green would be industrialised and partly ringed by hutments, displaying the Victorian zest for getting things done. Ashwell had laid out a work-yard in the handiest place, beside the Ingleton road. Service units included a blacksmith's shop and saw mill, carpenter's shed and stables, pay office and stores. Workshops were set up. Men and machines were assembled. Job Hirst's main concern was to have a sufficient number of masons who would dress and position on the viaduct the blocks of dark limestone he proposed to quarry.

Ashwell told F S Williams, historian of the Midland, that a considerable search had been made for a quarry. Trial holes were sunk. The best source was found beneath the bed of the beck in Littledale and from it were taken over 30,000 cubic yards of rock. A disadvantage of Littledale was that the quarries flooded when the beck was in spate. The water was eventually made to flow over the railway with the construction of a large stone trough lined with asphalt.

An urgent priority was the construction of tramways so that heavy objects, basically stone and coal, could be moved by rail. Into being came a locomotive workshop and a deep inspection pit, solidly stone-lined. Tramways patterned the area like veins on the back of a leaf. With the tramway system established on land rented from the Farrers, locomotives hauling strings of trucks handled incoming equipment on the road from Ingleton, transported quarried limestone from Littledale and supplied coal and bricks to Blea Moor.

A Victorian contractor, dependent as much on manpower as machines, needed gangers, time-keepers, brickmakers, carpenters, horse-keepers, carters, engine-drivers, stokers, tippers, saddlers, mechanics, sayers, quarrymen, cement burners, mortar grinders, engine tenders and – at the bottom of the list – a small army of indomitable, untutored, unskilled but indispensable navvies, the prime shifters of earth.

When the viaduct was completed, the huge embankments on either side would be created by systematic tipping of earth, using horses and carts. In construction work there was a clear distinction between two types – tip-horses and road-horses. A good horse was valued at 40 guineas. If a tip-horse were to lose its shoe, and a road-horse was substituted, it was not usually lively enough to avoid a runaway wagon. Such a horse, entangled in a rope, was run over by a wagon and had to be destroyed.

A special form of transport at Batty Green was the "bog cart", a light chassis fixed to a barrel, such as had been used agriculturally since the 18th century. It travelled smoothly over the wettest ground. The luckless horse that drew the cart ran the risk of breaking a limb.

The Bog Cart, devised to be horse-drawn over boggy ground. An illustration from F S Williams' history of the Midland Railway, which provides a contemporary account of building the Settle-Carlisle line.

What had been a quiet road from Ingleton became deeply scored by railhead traffic, including horse-drawn wagons bearing baulks of timber to provide staging for emergent piers on the viaduct. A local man complained: "After a good shower of rain, the streets and roads of the village [of Ingleton] are thick puddle...Thacking Road, leading to the Storrs limekilns, is broken up and worn into hollows, axle trees are broken and carts in other ways injured. The dale road has never been in so bad a state of repair within the memory of the oldest living inhabitant..."

A year later, the dale road was still in a mess, with "holes and ridges, ruts and hollows, pools of water and rolling mud." It had become dangerous for carriages, difficult for carting and almost impassable to pedestrians. A gentleman of long association with the road bemoaned its present state, which was so bad "I had to scale tottering walls, skip over rushing streams gushing gleesomely from the hillside, and walk over rugged pastures to avoid a road which, for its miserable condition, is almost as widely known as the far-famed Batty Wife Hole."

Job Hirst, having Littledale as a source of "black" limestone, taken from a low level where it was most durable, now concentrated on motivating the stonemasons who dressed the quarried blocks. It was done by "plug and feather", a wedge being driven into stone and hammered until that stone broke. Job's initial concern had been the foundations of the first set of piers. He restlessly visited the chosen spots where men dug to a depth of 25-ft to reach the carboniferous limestone.

A pier rested on a platform of concrete. A story is told that the viaduct was built on wool, which was not the case. Another story suggests that fleeces were set to lag the sides of the excavation. The fleece that kept a dale-country sheep snug and dry was, in effect, an ideal substitute for a dam. Perhaps.

The viaduct was to be constructed from north to south. The total number of arches would be decided two years after the work began. Everything would then depend on the relative size of two labour forces -- masons and embankment-tippers. Crossley had designed the viaduct so that each sixth pier would be ennobled as a "King Pier", being three times the thickness of the ordinary pier. Each arch would have a 45-ft span and 18-ft rise.

Over: There are only two known photographs of Ribblehead viaduct under construction, both dating from 1873. This view from the south-west looking towards Blea Moor shows the extensive use of timber scaffolding and platforms. The brickworks with its twin chimneys is to the immediate right of the completed scaffolding. Faintly visible on the extreme right are some of the huts in the shanty settlement.

The second known photograph looking south towards Ingleborough across Batty Moss. The abutment and seven of the stone piers have been completed and centring has been positioned for turning the arch rings in brick.

Opposite:

Top: Detail showing the complex timber staging.

Bottom: The illustration of Ribblehead viaduct in Williams' history of the Midland Railway is thought to have been drawn from the photograph depicting the works from the same angle.

The emergent piers were to be enfolded by a light timber stage. This supported a gantry on which ran a steam traveller – a mobile crane – which was capable of lifting a five ton stone to a height of 70-ft in two and a-half minutes. Two hand-cranes and their travellers turned pieces of stone and set them in place. In September, 1871, a fatality among the workforce was reported. As a three-ton stone was being raised by crane, David Davies, aged 32, went under the jib-end of the crane. The check-gearing broke off and struck him, fracturing his skull.

When the height of the masonry reached that of the gantry, a new lift of timber was added. The traveller and other equipment were then raised to the new height. To economise on timber needed for the staging, the viaduct was constructed in sections of seven piers at a time, beginning at the northern end. When the arches were turned, the scaffolding would be moved to the next set of seven. The new shafts had already attained a reasonable height.

Steam-powered crane used in building the viaduct.

Drawing from Williams' Midland Railway history of a Settle-Carlisle viaduct under construction.

The viaduct would absorb an estimated 30,000 cubic yards of masonry and 3,000 cubic yards of concrete. The mortar that bound stone to stone was mixed using a 10-hp engine. Local lime was not considered suitable. The contractor favoured Barrow lime from Leicestershire. The arches were formed of locally-made bricks and the voussoirs [facing stones] were of limestone.

Initially, Job Hirst had mustered 60 masons and labourers, a number that would rise to about 100. The turnover of workers was about eight a day. Good wages were paid but the men jibbed at being exposed to grim weather. Masons were at risk of being blown from the temporary decking by winds zipping up Chapel-le-Dale. Their fingers were cracked open at times of frost. They were placated when the contractor arranged for shelter to be provided. Masons at ground level worked in sheds that offered protection from wind and rain.

Batty Green had its own brickworks, managed by Robert Nixon, aided by brother John. Both men and their respective families hailed from Northampton – good brick-making country – and they had found living accommodation in Sebastopol, to the north-east of Batty Green. It was Home Sweet Home for a relatively short time. Robert's wife eloped with one Henry White. The couple were pursued by the police as far as Skipton, where all trace of them was lost. James Rixon, described as a brickmaker, was brought before the magistrates at Ingleton charged with assaulting a worker.

The arches of the viaduct would absorb one and a-half million bricks and yet more bricks – myriad bricks - were needed for lining and arching Blea Moor tunnel. A bed of clay lying under peat was a handy source of material. It was basically poor stuff, and much of it, being sandy, was discarded. It was at least handy and, by and large, free of limestone pebbles.

The brickworks employed up to 28 people. At its heart was a machine built by Porter & Company of Carlisle and reputed to be economical with fuel. There were ten ovens, each with two fire-holes. To make bricks, shale was ground, then mixed with the clay. An oven held from 14,000 to 15,000 bricks and it took a week to burn them. The bricks were said to be of such superior quality that when thrown out of the ovens they rang like pots. With local clay being used, this "ringing" aspect must have been an advertising ploy.

A traveller seventy yards long delivered bricks to a shed above the ovens where they were dried by the waste heat. Porter's machine when in full working state produced around 20,000 bricks a day. A visiting journalist saw two girls carrying bricks from the traveller, which worked incessantly.

Blea Moor tunnel was out of sight but not out of the mind of the denizens of Batty Green. By the autumn of 1871, about 150,000 cubic yards of material had been excavated at the southern side of Blea Moor to form cuttings. Two locomotives hauling tip wagons dumped the material where a steep bank would connect with the masonry on the northern side of the viaduct. Most of the work on the Blea Moor part of the line was let to gangs from Batty Green. The men divided their earnings equally among themselves or in proportion to the hours they worked.

Boulder clay, deposited in the glacial period, had a curious nature. If it was hard, it must be drilled and then blasted with gunpowder. Following a spell of rain, it became thick and gluey, so adhesive and tough that when a navvy stuck his pickaxe into it he could hardly get it out again. An engineer reported seeing sixteen displaced tip-wagons that had been displaced when in the process of discharging their load; they would have slipped much further but for a bulling-chain placed between the tip-rails which, the moment the wagon tipped its load, ensured that the wagon was pulled up and prevented from following.

F S Williams, the indispensable Midland historian, noted that "even when it has come out as dry rock and been put into the tip-wagon, a shower of rain, or even the jolting of a ride of a mile to the tip end, will perhaps shake the whole into a nearly semi-fluid mass of 'slurry', which settles down like glue to the bottom of the wagon, and when run to the 'tip head' will drag the wagon over to the bottom of the embankment."

In late March, 1871, the whole district shook. An earthquake was experienced, the effect being felt throughout Lancashire and Yorkshire and as far north as Scotland. A slight shock was reported at 6 p.m. Tremors were more severe during the night. A correspondent of the Lancaster Guardian noted: "It cannot but be amusing to learn what impression the earthquake made on the inhabitants of the huts on the wild moorland of Blea Moor."

Many were aroused from their slumbers "and at a loss to account for the midnight disturber of their slumbers. One of the ladies at Jericho compared the noise that preceded the shaking with the rumbling of a train through a tunnel in a town. Another, who awoke from her rest, got up to find what was wrong, but failing to ascertain the cause, her lodgers went out with lanterns to discover the shaker of their hut in vain. At last they found that the door latch was deranged but failed to detect the invisible agent who had tampered with it."

The hostess of a hut at Jericho thought the shock was caused by "the bursting of an engine that was close by." In another hut, the bed shook "so that the fair occupant in her fright got hold of the bed-posts." An indescribable noise that attended the earthquake caused general alarm.

On a summer's day, in 1870, John Ashwell supervised the delivery of a new locomotive that had been kept overnight at Ingleton. It had been brought to the village by the Midland. The only way to transport it to Batty Wife Hole was to yolk to it a large number of horses. Job Hirst was among those who watched it being transported to Batty Green, the journey beginning at Ingleton at about 3 a.m.

A correspondent of the Lancaster Guardian noted that with a monster steam engine on its way to Batty Wife Hole, the street was packed with people and obstructed by carters and horses. That night, it required fourteen strong horses and the assistance of a large number of men to get the engine above Storrs. "To the credit of Mr Moody, who was in charge of Mr Ashwell's horses, he would not allow a whip to be used."

Artist's impression of a contractor's locomotive being transported from Ingleton to Batty Green.

The horses, with the assistance of the men, each of whose exertions had been stimulated by the promise of a pint of beer, drew the monster machine up the hill and on the following day they managed, in the early morning, with a team of twenty-four horses, to get the engine to the summit of a steep hill on the other side of Chapel-le-Dale. The rest of the journey was on the level...

In the following June, the routine was repeated with another railway engine. "The tramp of Mr Ashwell's sleek-skinned and well-fed horses warned many of the people that if they wished to see the removal of the engine from the Back gate, their snug quarters must be quitted without delay." Over thirty horses were yoked up to the locomotive for the ascent of the Storrs. "It was a fine sight to see so many horses willingly exert themselves to draw the ponderous machine. Though the hour of departure was early, many women as well as men accompanied the lengthy team to above the Storrs. It was well for both man and beast that the weather was so fine, or the imperfect state of the road would have made the transit of the engine a difficult matter."

It was virtually Ashwell's last fling. As long ago as 3 May, 1970, he had been summoned by the chairman of the Construction Committee to a meeting at which the dissatisfaction felt by the directors was expressed. Ashwell had made little progress with works in his contract; the necessity for increased exertion was urged upon him. He had promised this should be made. Later in the month the solicitors were instructed "to prepare and serve a notice on Mr Ashwell requiring him to find and provide such additional machinery, plant and labour as Mr Crossley shall consider necessary in order to expedite the progress of the works at the Blea Moor tunnel with a view to their completion within the time specified..."

Crossley reported on 4 July that Contract No 1 was moving a little further. "Tramway formed from Ingleton road to south face of tunnel...Numerous pieces of machinery now in situ, including 4 locomotives, 440 wagons, 3 winding engines, 3 portable cranes and 2 steam cranes." Ashwell had suffered, as did other contractors, from shortage of labour, which retarded work and missed deadlines.

He had by far the most arduous of the three mainline contracts. He requested the Midland to loan him money, which they did. He still did not have the funds to complete the job. In October, 1871, the contract was cancelled. John Ashwell had done his best, which was not good enough. The Midland directors recognised he had under-estimated costs.

He left their employ with a handshake. The sums involved must have amazed local people. He had borrowed a total of £50,000. He was paid £10,000 in discharge. The Midland took over the work by direct labour. The man appointed to oversee Contract No 1 was William H Ashwell, who was unrelated to the previous contractor. Through him, the company undertook to complete the contract.

Chapter Four

Workers arrive from near and far – Job Hirst and his family settle in – Bed and board in the shanty huts – Hymns of praise and jugs of ale – A smallpox summer.

The 1871 census for Ingleton Fells new parish recorded an upsurge in the railway population. Work-hardened men from all parts of Britain were lured to North Ribblesdale by relatively high wages and the appeal of steady work for several years. A fair proportion of the immigrants knew little else but railway building. Among them were men with extravagant names: Belter, Punch and Pincer.

A Welsh mason needed little instruction when given a job on the viaduct. A Derbyshire lead-miner was at ease when working in the confines of Blea Moor tunnel. A Nottinghamshire man had been brought up in a brick-making community and needed little tuition at Batty Green. In a richly diverse labour force, the most prized workers were masons, miners and those who would produce bricks (of a sort) for viaduct and tunnel. For the man brought up in a village near Taunton in Somerset, the transition from an agricultural life to an existence in a "shanty" at Blea Moor must have been traumatic.

Thomas Porter, better known as Blind Tom, a blaster who had been blinded while working was on the bridge over the Menai Strait, Anglesey, was among the applicants for work. His mates had a collection and bought a donkey and cart for him and his Welsh-speaking wife so that (slowly) they might make their way to Ribblehead. Tom got employment. He was blasting again! His procedure was to work out the length and time of a fuse by counting knots in a length of rope. His wife took in lodgers, brewed ale and was a local midwife.

The least-prized workers were locals, who were not dependable, slipping back to their villages and farms during such busy times as lambing and haytime. Conversely, a farmer with time on his hands and a horse and cart handy was able to find employment carting stone and other heavy materials at the railway works.

Labour being scarce and difficult to retain, a wage of 10s a day became general for skilled men. If the masons went on strike – which they did – they were almost certain to earn extra cash. John Crossley, in one of his regular reports to the Construction Committee, commented that workmen "stay their hours but do not work to hurt themselves." A man who found good lodgings would send for wife and family.

Victorian lead-miners at Nenthead, who in their manner and clothing would differ little from railway navvies.

Mrs Mitchell, of the Isle of Dogs, Poplar, left London with four children to join her husband, William, a railway labourer. When she arrived by train at Ingleton she found that Matilda, one of the children, was dead. The child was a surviving twin, ten weeks old, and had been ailing from birth. There was no surprise that the child had died suddenly. Being among strangers, the grieving mother said nothing to anyone about her dead child but got transport to Chapel-le-Dale and the farm of John Morphet, Lower Scales, where her husband was reportedly staying. He had gone to lodge at one of the huts near Batty Wife Hole.

In the first year of serious construction work, the number of huts between Batty Moss and Dent Head was over 150. According to the 1871 census, up to 1,000 people were residing in the area. At Batty Wife Hole, which had the largest number of huts, the residents numbered 344. Medical facilities were provided. A doctor's services were needed. Huts situated on bogland were overcrowded, ill drained and the resort of rats which "had jovial doings amongst the hut inhabitants. For their plentiful keep they are much given to nightly romping above the ceilings."

Batty Green – one of a series of drawings by the artist Betty Harrington.

The chirp of the house sparrow had not been heard at isolated Gearstones before the huts on Blea Moor were erected. "Rambler", in the Lancaster Guardian, wrote: "Now the landlord of the inn is much annoyed on account of their interference with his pet martins, who in large numbers build their nests under the eaves of his house and of his outbuildings."

Families who found accommodation and wholesome food at local farms had cause to rejoice. John Maud, a mason's labourer, boarded with the Bentham family at Winterscales. William Jackson, quarryman, and his wife Sarah, who hailed from Sedbergh and Liverpool respectively, lodged at Dowbiggins. William Mill and Alexander Gordon, two out-of-work masons from Scotland, were at the time of the 1871 census boarding with Robert Lodge at Newby Head, which was then an inn as well as a farmhouse, situated on the watershed at an elevation of 1,400-ft above sea level.

Ingleton in about 1865, a few years before it became the major supply point for the construction of Ribblehead viaduct. The more modest structure in the background formed a link in the Midland's first bid to reach Scotland, the failure of which led to the building of the Settle-Carlisle line.

There was Census mention of Batty Wife Hole, Sebastopol, Six Huts, Jericho, Jordan and the huts situated on Blea Moor. Mention of Inkerman and Belgravia occurred in the parish registers of Chapel-le-Dale. Batty Wife Hole was not exclusively residential. Apart from some of the best huts there was a saddler's shop, a grocer's shop, a shoemaker's shop, four greengrocers and a shop retailing books and stationery. A brewery was a welcome addition. The prospect of having a large "tommy" shop was alluring.

At Ingleton, the major supply point, streets echoed, by day and night, to the rattle of tradesmen's carts heading to Batty Green with greens and roots from the vegetable markets of Leeds, Manchester and Lancaster. Hawkers and traders converged on the area like bees around a honeypot. The Lancaster Guardian noted in March, 1871, that the Lancaster and Richmond turnpike road [the main route through Chapel-le-Dale] had holes and ridges, ruts and hollows, pools of water and rolling mud. It was, in truth, "dangerous for carriages, difficult for carting, and almost impassable for pedestrians."

Overnight accommodation was available for strangers. A commercial visitor who had been to Blea Moor "passed through thick heather to Gearstones Inn, where I met with substantial fare and comfortable lodgings at moderate charges." In Wildman's Household Almanack there was mention of migrant traders at Batty Green – potters, drapers, dairymen, greengrocers, butchers, bakers, all with horses and carts, and in addition brewers' drays. Numerous hawkers on foot "plied from hut to hut their different trades."

There's an old Yorkshire saying: "It's your stomach 'as 'ods your back up." Good food, in substantial quantities, was available to sustain the railway families. A note written in 1871 recorded: "Though the hut villages of Batty Green, Sebastopol and Jericho are upon a dreary moor far away from the busy marts of commercial men, still there was no lack of roast beef, savoury pastry, luscious fruits and beverages of pleasant flavour to the lovers of the bottle."

An up-and-coming firm was Messrs Burgoyne & Cocks, of Settle (Variants of the surname Burgoyne appeared in local records). The firm had a branch at Batty Wife Hole. Smaller shops were located at Stainforth, Helwith Bridge, Horton-in-Ribblesdale, Selside, Ashes, Sebastopol, Jericho, Tunnel Huts and Dent Head. Each week, four fat cows and a dozen or so sheep were slaughtered and the meat retailed. At Settle, using two large ovens, the firm turned out 4,000 loaves – daily. At Batty Green, a brick oven was used to produce 2,000 loaves.

Four horses were kept to haul the carts that delivered goods to the firm's shops. Burgoyne and Cocks also dealt in newspapers and weekly periodicals. Among these were 80 copies of Police News, 80 Budgets, 40 to 50 Family Herald and 36 copies of a local newspaper, Lancaster Guardian, which matched the interest and reported extensively on local happenings. In 1871, so successful was the enterprise that the firm moved to new premises in Duke Street, Settle. A journalist noted: "This establishment is a great improvement to the street and on this account the firm last week gave their customers 500 glass cream jugs and sugar basins."

There were local shortages, such as with footwear. Only two "shoemakers" plied their trade at Batty Green in 1871. Presumably, there were many civilian shoe and bootmakers in the area. That summer, a post office was opened, the mail – collected from a train at Clapham – being brought up from Ingleton.

A cause of postal annoyance was the fact that for a time letter-bags lay at Clapham station, to be forwarded or not, as might happen, by the first goods train or later passenger train to Ingleton. One day, the morning letters reached the village after dark, the night mail having already been despatched. Promises by the postal authority to improve the service "ended in moonshine or worse."

Mr Ashwell, the contractor, told the post-messenger that if he would fetch the letter bags from Clapham, he would pay for the extra labour. The postal authority objected. No payment should be made to a private individual in addition to his salary. Asked to name a sum, the postman mentioned 1s daily and 4d for his fare to Clapham by the first train. It was considered exorbitant. The remuneration was fixed at 1s, including expenses. So the poor man was paid fourpence for a four-mile ride, twopence for each letter-bag and one penny for walking each mile on the return route.

The huts raised on and around Batty Green were of several standard sizes, the largest having three rooms. Weatherproofing was achieved by spreading boiling tar over every joint on the felt that covered the roof. On Contract No 1, it was estimated that enough felt was used to make a path six feet wide along the entire length of the new line. Furnishings were adequate but crude. Some wives brightened up the inner walls with pictures taken from newspapers or magazines. The standard rate for lodgers, 13s a week, incorporated a night's sleep, breakfast and washing.

Mealtime in a navvy family's hut, as imagined by Betty Harrington.

No 1 Batty Wife Hole was allocated to the Holland family, who hailed from Lincolnshire. When first heard of, Robert, the head of the family, was a railway labourer, aged 48. He was married to Elizabeth, aged 43, their daughters - Mary, Anne, Susan, Betsy and Rebecca – being aged respectively, 18, 15, 12, 10, 6. All had been born when dad was working in Northampton.

The Hollands managed to pack into their hut lodgers with Northampton links. They were officially termed "boarders", their ages ranging from 20 to 56. As early as May, 1870, Robert sought permission, at the Petty Sessions in May, to be considered at the forthcoming Brewster Sessions for a licence to sell strong drink. If this had been agreed, a proper licence would have been issued, but he did not get the Bench's recommendation for want of signatures to his petition.

An insight into life in his hut at Batty Wife Hole was given at Ingleton Court, in June, 1872, when Robert, now described as a provision dealer, was charged – on the information of the police – with selling drink without a licence. On the bench were James Farrer and John T Rice. Robert had no advocate.

The case for the prosecution, presented by Supt Exton, was based on evidence given by Thomas Cryer who, with John White and Samuel Paradise, entered Holland's house about 8 p.m. They had joined between 20 and 30 people, some of whom were dancing, others singing, and judging by glasses on the table, some were drinking. When Cryer called for a pint of beer, it was promptly supplied by Mrs Holland. He paid her threepence for it. The beer was drunk, to be followed by several more glasses. These were enjoyed by both him and his friends. Cryer had seen no-one else pay for drink. And all he paid was the initial threepence.

Evidence for Cryer was given by Elizabeth Parsons, who had entered the building at about 10 p.m., when – she affirmed - there were about seven men, and as many young women, in the house. She reported that when the complainant "kicked up a row", he was put out of the house by Mrs Holland but, going to the back door, he re-entered, only to be turned out a second time. She had not seen anyone pay for either wine or beer. She had drunk a little wine.

William Stafford, who lodged with the Holland family, was in the house, though not in the same room, when Cryer arrived. That evening, he did not see him drink any beer. He corroborated the last witness's evidence as to the complainant making a disturbance and being turned out thrice on that account by Mrs Holland. The young folk were in festive mood. The daughter of a Mrs Flower, an acquaintance of the Misses Holland, had come down from London, and Mrs Holland was treating them. The Bench suspended its decision on the case until the hearing of assault that arose from it.

Robert Holland now entered the story; he had arrived home at about 10-30 p.m and told the obstreperous Thomas Cryer "I'll shift you." Opening the door, he set his bulldog on him. The dog tried to seize Thomas by the throat. He kept it off by his hand, which it bit in several places.

Holland told the Bench he did not want a row and Cryer was kicking his house door. He had been fighting on the moor and his mistress had been obliged to turn him out. Cryer denied that he had fought that day.

Samuel Paradise had gone into the hut about 9-30 p.m. The young man (Cryer) was singing. Mrs Holland said she did not want any of his noise and showed him the door. He kicked the door but was not admitted. Shortly afterwards, Mr Holland returned home and said that he would shift him. Which he did – with the help of the bulldog. Both cases were dismissed.

The official story was fictionalised, the surname Holland changed to Pollen, and published in Chamber's Journal under the title A Navvies Ball. In this admittedly very entertaining story, Pollen had taken a letter for the writer down to Ingleton. In the afternoon, the writer of the story looked in to see whether he had come back. His good lady reported his non-arrival, adding: "Afore we comed here, we were on the 'Surrey and Sussex'." That morning, Betsy Smith, "a lass as my daughter knowed there", came to the hut to see her mother, who was married to old Recks, "and my girls, they be to have a holiday for to spend wi' their old friend."

She "bid them tighten themselves up a bit, and tak' a basket and go to the top of Ingleborough Hill, the three on 'em, for a day's 'scursion like; and when they'd come back, I'd have tea waitin' an; a cake, and I'd get in a bottle or two of wine, and we'd make a bit of a feast on't, you see, sir, for the lasses mayn't see one another no more in this here life." The writer was invited into the hut, where he might join in the modest festivities of the evening. "Why, it was the very thing I desired."

The "lasses" had by now got down from Ingleborough and were seated round a huge coal-fire in Mrs Pollen's keeping-room. "It was a state occasion; and the six navvies, who are lodgers, were relegated to their own sleeping apartment, where I found Mr Pollen, slightly the fresher from his journey to Ingleton, and having his hair cut by one of the lodgers prior to entering the sphere of gentility in the other room."

Mrs Pollen was "painfully polite and her notions of my capacities for rashers of bacon eaten along with buttered toast must have been based on her experience of navvies. The young ladies were at first slightly distrait, but Ingleborough air had given their appetite a beautiful fillip. Mr Pollen was benignly jocose, with a slight tendency to hiccup." He gave an entertaining account of navvy life as it applied to the railway works. The story took in the spontaneous dancing and the turfing out several times of an awkward interloper.

Through Pollen, plus his family, boarders and friends, we have some vivid word-pictures [written in 1873, which was "railway time"] of a navvy population that did not keep fashionable hours and took every opportunity for enjoyment. There was a tap at the door communicating with the room inhabited by the navvy lodgers. "Sundry smothered and gasping squeakings of a fiddle had been audible lately from that apartment. The "lasses" who had climbed a mountain were yawning a little after tea. As the tap at the door was heard, the young ladies smiled and Mrs Pollen called "Come in."

A stalwart navvy entered the room, his powerful frame contrasting comically with his shamefaced countenance. He was blushing from ear to ear, yet there was a twinkle in the big black eye of this good-looking fellow. He bore a message from the navvies in the other room: might they be allowed to join the festivities? Pollen agreed. His wife only stipulated that they behaved themselves.

"The navvies trooped solemnly in and seated themselves on the extreme edge of a form. Mrs Pollen helped them to wine...Then the black-eyed navvy took her aside, an interview which resulted in the introduction of a pail of strong ale and a bottle of whisky. The navvies were a decided acquisition."

Saturday night at Batty Green (Drawn by Betty Harrington).

The black-eyed navvy, having switched his position to one between Mrs Pollen and the lass from the "Surrey and Sussex" played a lively spring on his fiddle. Tom Purgin, "a smart ruddy-faced young fellow with black curling hair and the physical development of a Hercules", sang My Pretty Jane.

A dance followed. It was "something between a reel and an Irish jig". The black-eyed navvy distinguished himself by playing and dancing simultaneously. His big boots made a thunderous noise, especially in the double-shuffle. The beer-pail was replenished. The evening was passing hilariously. At a loud knock on the outdoor, Mrs Pollen admitted a stranger. He was a big navvy in working clothes. He named himself the Wellingborough Pincer, from Northamptonshire, as was Pollen. He had come to pay his respects and was conspicuously drunk.

Allowed to stay, he resorted "with marked freedom and frequency to the beer-can." The other navvies could do no more than tolerate his bad behaviour but his conduct was leading to a shindy. Mrs Pollen, who had been out of the room, serving some customers at their little shop, returned and comprehended that trouble as well as ale was brewing. "In two strides, she had the Wellingborough Pincer by the scruff of the neck and was bundling him towards the door. He struggled a little, but Mrs Pollen pinioned him with a vice-like grasp." Promptly, dexterously she ejected him from the hut.

Harmony was restored, for a time. Mrs Pollen had not bolted the door. He reappeared on the scene and entered, bent on apologising for his bad conduct. His apparent sincerity was accepted "but his apparent contrition seemed linked with a keen anxiety to return to the neighbourhood of the beer-pail."

Without warning, he hit Tom Purgin in the eye. Tom, wiping some blood from his cheek-bone, showed self-restraint, remarking that it would "keep till tomorrow." The Pincer had gone too far and was grasped by Mrs Pollen, dragged across the floor and ejected once again. The Pincer hammered on the door and window-shutters of the hut. He shouted abuse. Mrs Pollen restrained her navvy boarders, who were keen to tackle him.

Mr Pollen, inebriated, rose slowly to his feet and shouted "Joe!" A powerfully built bulldog appeared from under the table and accompanied Pollen to the door, just as Pincer recommenced pounding it with blows of his fists. "'Here, Joe' was all Pollen's reply to the volley of execrations that greeted him. There was a dull thud of a heavy fall, a gurgling noise and at Pollen's word, 'Come, Joe!' the dog reappeared, sententiously wagging his tail. The door was shut. The Wellingborough Pincer demonstrated no more against it."

The Pincer responded by contacting the police. Two summonses were issued. One was for selling drink without a licence [the subject of the original news item] and the other was for setting a dog on Pincer. In the court case, judgement went against the Pincer on both counts. He had to pay costs. Pincer returned to work but was shunned by the whole community.

He was last seen in the neighbourhood of a deep blind shaft that had been excavated to divert the water from the workings in Blea Moor tunnel. "He may have suddenly migrated, but there are not wanting those who darkly hint that an exploration of the shaft would disclose the fact of his being in the immediate vicinity of its bottom."

So much for No 1 Batty Wife Hole, residence of the Hollands (nee Pollen). In No 2 Batty Wife Hole lived our hero, Job Hirst, designated as "railway sub-contractor". Living with him was Mary his wife, with four sons. Charles H and Walter H, railway labourers, were aged 21 and 19 respectively. Joshua Hirst, aged 16, was a carpenter. William, their son, and daughter Nancy were still of school age. Job's nomadic life was implied by the birth places of the younger members of his family – Newport, South Wales, Trimpington in Cambridge and St Pancras, Middlesex.

Job, a sociable type of man, was soon on cordial terms with his neighbours, especially James Tiplady, the denizen of Hut No 3, Batty Wife Hole. He was an affable missionary, emissary of Bradford Town Mission, selected by the Midland directors out of 200 applicants. In acknowledgement, they donated £200 a year to the Mission. In the same hut as Mr Tiplady were Jane Herbert, schoolmistress, described as "boarder"; she hailed from Stratford on Avon. Also 16-year-old Eliza Combs, a native of Portsmouth, classified as "domestic servant".

Mr Tiplady was to recall: "I commenced my labours here on 16 June, 1870, and as long as the weather permitted, in addition to visiting the huts, I continued holding services in the open-air. The congregation at these services were credible to the people and highly encouraging to myself." He was expected to have in mind the whole 17 miles of Contract No 1. Mr William Fletcher was appointed missionary to the railway workers further north.

Tiplady's duties included conducting services at Dent Head, where a Mission Room was established. At times, he had the company of a visiting preacher. They stopped, where convenient, at the various settlements. At Tunnel Huts, they came across an Irishman who was quietly, reverently, reading the Book of Common Prayer.

Tiplady recorded: "He is a common workman with a large family in Ireland and still I was told that he is in the habit of sending a sovereign weekly to his family. When asked how he could do it, to his honour and good sense he said he could not think of spending his money on drink and let his wife and children at home be in want." Tiplady added: "If reading the Prayer Book on Sunday on a barren moor, when a man is cut off from a place of worship, leads a man to thus remember his distant family, it would be well if more railway operatives would go and do likewise."

Tiplady had to restrict his activities when "the winter set in with great severity and as open-air services could no longer be held...Recently, I have opened a room at Batty Wife for Sunday afternoon and evening services, which are well attended and which was kindly erected for me by W

H Ashwell, Esq., contractor. Here we have established a Sunday school and contemplate also a day school, if a master can be found to come and live in this wild and mountainous district."

Living at No 4 Batty Wife Hole was George Capstick, book-keeper, and his family. At No 5 resided Francis Moody, "overlooker on railway works" and his family. Job Hirst's wife became friendly, for personal reasons, with the Tebbulls of Hut No 45. Loisa Tebbull was a seamstress, her daughters Louisa and Sarah being dressmakers. There was a visiting milliner. On special occasions, Mary Hirst need not look dowdy.

Batty Wife Hole did not score many points on the social scale. Most of the tenants were railway labourers. Other trades and occupations represented were fireman on railway, engine driver, sawyer, blacksmith, blacksmith's striker, wheelwright, carpenter, butcher, warehouseman, grocer's shopman, stone mason, horsekeeper, farrier, shoemaker, tailor, baker, clerk, saddler, grocer and timekeeper.

The much larger settlement of Sebastopol lay on the edge of Batty Moss. This and the mysterious Inkerman had been named after victories in the Crimean War. It could be that one or two men who turned up for work at Batty Green had helped to construct a railway in the Crimea along which stores landed by sea were speedily transported to the front-line.

The most surprising name, Belgravia, was doubtless a tongue-in-cheek allusion to a better-class London district. Or perhaps it was because it stood on the north-east side of Sebastopol. The huts of Belgravia were slightly better class, with porches, and would be occupied by the managerial class.

The hutments known as Jericho and Jerusalem not only reflected names from the Bible but were geographically correct. One went up the hill from Jericho to Jerusalem; higher still to reach a scratch collection of shacks on Blea Moor that were simply known as Tunnel Huts.

Overcrowding appeared to be the rule on the Dent side of Blea Moor. David Page, Medical Officer of Health for Sedbergh, reported that the cubic space to each occupant in the sleeping apartments was very much below the minimum required for the maintenance of health. "In one hut I noticed five besteads jammed so tightly together that the sleepers in reaching the farthest beds must necessarily clamber over the others." A Methodist local preacher who visited Blea Moor in 1872 noticed, while passing these huts, that pigs, ducks and hens wandered at large on the moor, "showing that the railway operatives, however unfavourably circumstanced, cannot rest without they are surrounded with the domestic animals."

Tiplady began his missionary work at Batty Wife Hole on 16 June, 1870, with the awesome task of covering the 17 miles of No 1 Contract, from Settle to Dent Head. He concentrated on Batty Green and its satellites, visiting the huts and holding religious services in the open air at Batty Wife, Sebastopol and Denthead.

A mission room was the focal point for this work. The plainness of the mission's walls was offset by "pictorial embellishment" stressing the virtues of thrift and kindness. The room was heated by large stoves and across one end was a platform with a rostrum from which Mr Tiplady preached the Gospel. Space was available in this raised area for Gospel Singers to perform. The Flock doubtless enjoyed the hymns of two popular American evangelists, Moody and Sankey, and – with the grandeur of the Three Peaks around them – would render with gusto 'Go Tell it to the Mountain'.

Batty Green mission provided food for both mind and body. In March, 1871, a hundred people attended a tea party at which there was more than enough food available. "Large heaps and fragments were left." Tiplady hoped that if a schoolmaster could be found to settle in "this wild and mountainous district" a day school would be a possibility. "The people are, with few exceptions, a good-hearted, generously-disposed class, glad to receive instruction and very attentive to what is said." Miss Herbert, schoolmistress, taught at such a school when it was opened shortly; she had 43 scholars who were reportedly clean, neatly attired "and on account of their docility and good behaviour a credit to their parents and the railway public."

Children at the outer hutments were neglected. A visitor in the autumn of 1871 saw "groups of children here and there". The children sat on the moor, "which must, on account of its swampy condition, be very injurious to their health. Surely the Midland Company might do something towards the education of those neglected children who through the circumstances of the workmen are deprived of the educational advantages of towns and villages."

Mr Tiplady did not remain long at Batty Green. In February, 1872, he moved to the Midland line at Chesterfield. The Lancaster Guardian reported that "as Mr Tiplady was wearied of his lonely position, he a few days ago bid farewell to bachelordom at Bradford and in consequence of the delightful step he had taken, his friends at Batty Green resolved to furnish him with some useful article as a token of their high esteem."

He had arrived a bachelor; he was now leaving as a married man, with the thanks of many friends. Such thanks were voiced by our old friend Job Hirst, sub-contractor. Tiplady's successor, one Henry Hancock, handed him a farewell gift, which was a cruet set "in the name of the numerous subscribers to the testimonial."

Events were organised at Batty Green to raise money for a tablet to be placed in Chapel-le-Dale church "in remembrance of the poor workmen who have lost their lives by accident on the Settle-Carlisle railway." A concert was followed by a grand ball, from which the dancers did not disperse until 6 a.m. Another concert, sponsored by Messrs Burgoyne and Cocks, bakers and provision merchants, raised funds for Leeds Infirmary.

In typical Victorian fashion, the Midland and its contractor diverted the men's attention from undesirable activities. As early as 1871, Penny Readings were being held each week at Batty Green; the object was "to attract the working classes from pursuits and places of a corrupting character." Local dignitaries supported and took part in these social events. T H Burgoyne composed and read The Batty Green Disaster. It dealt with:

A handsome, smart young grocer –
His name was William White –
He put the horse into the cart,
Which suddenly took fright.
(presumably the horse rather than the cart)

The fear of danger none can tell,
Round William's heart had stole,
As he neared that awful precipice
Which is known as Batty's Hole.
(horse, cart and William fell into the hole)

Assistance came; full five strong men
To move the cart which stuck like lead;
Poor William White sat trembling there
Upon the horse's head.
(horse and cart were rescued and comfortably re-united)

With songs and recitations, an audience was exposed, through variety in the tone of the items, to the gamut of emotion, from sadness to elation. In the unlikely setting of the hutment known as Jerusalem, where space for a public event must have been at a premium, people watched with lower jaws drooping in astonishment as a workman carried a hurdy-gurdy about the room and played a polka, "which had a very exciting influence on some of the women, who could not keep their feet still." Attending this concert was a contingent from Batty Green who subsequently walked back along the tramway as far as Sebastopol, thence "by the nearest way" to their homes. The most daunting part of the journey was the crossing of a wooden bridge where, not long before, a train with provisions had come to grief. The revellers found openings between the sleepers "wide enough for a corpulent boniface to drop through."

Mr Ashwell was benevolent but none the less managed to retain Victorian class-consciousness. When he presided over a Penny Reading in the Mission Room, he observed: "There is honour due to the Batty Wife Greeners inasmuch as they are able to furnish such talent from the lower and working classes." Talent was imported from Settle in the springtime of 1873. It was the last entertainment of the season, raising money for the National Lifeboat Institution.

The party from Settle arrived in the afternoon. An engine and carriage constructed for the occasion was placed at their disposal, running via Jericho, Inkerman and Sebastopol to the south portal of Blea Moor Tunnel. All the gentlemen and some of the more venturesome ladies descended a shaft into the tunnel.

In March, 1874, another talented Settle group visited the area. The schoolroom at Batty Green was the venue of a concert given by "some ladies and gentlemen, amateurs from Settle." The glee Huntsman's Chorus, by the company, opened the concert, and it ended on a wistful note when Misses Nelson and Hardacre, Messrs Overing and Hamilton, sang Ye Banks and Braes. Of special interest to those in the audience who had been experiencing a grim winter, near the 1,000-ft contour, was a song, Sunny Days Will Come Again.

There might have been one or two restless folk when Mr A Overing's special contribution was a song entitled Give Me an Honest Man. Henry Hancock, who thanked "the ladies and gentlemen engaged", mentioned the good cause for which the concerts were given, namely the erection of a memorial tablet in Chapel-le-Dale Church "in the remembrance of those poor workmen who have lost their lives by accident on the Settle and Carlisle Railway (Contract No 1)."

In November of that year, a grand concert was given in the Schoolroom, raising £10 16s for Leeds Infirmary. A front seat cost 2s.6d and the second seats 1s. A review of the programme appeared under Batty Green in the next issue of the Lancaster Guardian. "Every piece in the programme was rendered so effectively that it called forth the admiration and plaudits of the crowded audience. Perhaps the most impressive and pathetic piece was When Evening's Twilight, which was listened to with breathless silence."

The services of doctors were often required. Doctors were not immune from misfortune. In the summer of 1871, during a thunderstorm, Dr Griffiths set off from Batty Green to Ingleton, where his professional services were needed. A young man had been thrown from a horse, injuring his head. The doctor's horse, startled by a flash of lightning, reared up, the rider being thrown to the ground. He was able to remount and resume his journey.

The first ambulance to be introduced at Batty Green, in the earliest days, was horse-drawn, resembling one of the "covered wagons" familiar for many years to travellers on our roads and made internationally famous when the design was adapted for use on the plains of the American West. A temporary wooden structure was available as a first-aid station. It was barely adequate when, in

The ambulance at Batty Green had affinities with the American covered wagon.

the spring and summer of 1871, smallpox was rife in the hutments of Batty Green, being "painfully prevalent" at Sebastopol and Jericho.

The viral disease is believed to have been brought to the district in May by a man who complained of being feverish and with an aching head. An unsightly rash followed. Smallpox swept the hutments of Sebastapol and Jericho. Mr Ashwell, contractor, erected at his own expense two detached buildings of the ordinary hut size as a temporary smallpox hospital to accommodate ten patients. This was on condition that the Board of Guardians fitted it out, with the exception of bedsteads, and maintained it at their own cost.

The medical officer of this temporary smallpox and fever hospital at Batty Green was Edwin S Green, LRCP, &c. The clerk of the Guardians who helped to erect the hospital also issued notices relating to vaccination and re-vaccination, free of charge, to all over the whole works. Managing the hospital were Mr and Mrs Halifax, "two efficient trained nurses". The number of patients doubled when a covered way, 20-ft long, and yet another hut, this time 48-ft long, were added.

Page 30.

BURIALS in the Parish of Chapel le Dale or Ingleton Fells in the County of York in the Year 1871

Name.	Abode.	When buried.	Age.	By whom the Ceremony was performed.
William Dean No. 233.	Sebastopool	Jan. 22	11 month	Wm Harper
John Hollerenshaw No. 234.	Sebastopool	Jan 24	40 years	Wm Harper
Charles Bibby No. 235.	Sebastopool	Jan. 31	9 months	Wm Harper
Lorissa Annie Thompson No. 236.	Jericho	Feb. 1	3 years	Wm Harper
Fredrick Little No. 237.	Inkerman	Feb. 5	4 years	Wm Harper
Tom Atkinson Little No. 238.	Inkerman	Feb. 9	1 year & six month	Wm Harper
Thomas Smith No. 239.	Jericho	Feb. 12	10 months	Wm Harper
Ellen Higgins No. 240.	Blacmoor	March 26	1 year & 7 months	Wm Harper

Above: A page from the Burial Register at St Leonard's, Chapel-le-Dale. Note the high infant mortality.

Left: Details from the Burial Register with a mention of Batty Green and a note of the death of a four-month old boy.

Page 44.

BURIALS in the Parish of Chapel le Dale or Ingleton Fells in the County of York in the Year 1873.

Name.	Abode.	When buried.	Age.	By whom the Ceremony was performed.
William Goddard No. 345.	"Jericho" Railway Works	May 4th	4 months	Ar: Ashworth Offg. Min:
William Thomas No. 346.	Batty Green	May 22nd Ascension Day	32 years	Ar: Ashworth Offg. Min.

Funeral at St Leonard's (Betty Harrington).

A male nurse joined the staff. The infected huts were lime-washed, the clothes of patients were "baked" in a large oven and garments were washed and disinfected on the premises. A small library was provided for those who wished to read "during the somewhat tedious time of convalescence."

Some folk blamed intemperance for most of the fatal cases in adults. The Ingleton magistrates were criticised for granting too many licences to vendors of beers and spirits. Living conditions, being restricted and unsanitary, had been the cause of the spread. The Rev E Smith, vicar of Chapel-le-Dale, officiated at five funerals in a week. From one hut at Sebastopol were carried the bodies of a mother and three children. The Midland granted £20 towards the enlargement of the burial ground. This was consecrated in August. A lych-gate was added.

By July 10, the number of cases admitted to the hospital had risen to 35. Of these, nineteen were cured and released. Thirteen remained. By June, it was reported that no death had occurred at Batty Green for a fortnight. Those who caught the disease, and were now in hospital, responded favourably to treatment and good nursing. Soon, however, an upsurge in the number of cases led to four more deaths – two of children at Jericho and two of men who had been moved to the hospital.

The smallpox threat held everyone's attention for nearly three months. It affected workers on each of the contracts. The partnership of Bayliss & Eckersley on Contract 4 broke up under financial strain. The labour force along the line fell to under 6,000 and contractors had difficulty in maintaining numbers. Serious doubts arose about the completion of the railway in the specified time.

There was a moment of shock, followed by laughter, as the disease waned. A party of "gentlemen" visiting the hospital at Batty Green in 1874 were shown the "dead house", where one of the party lifted the lid of a coffin and found a fully-clothed body lying face downwards. He pinched a leg to ensure he was truly dead – and was startled when the "corpse" awoke, having been sleeping off a heavy drinking session. After asking for money, so he might buy more ale, he arose, walked and was last seen heading towards Keighley.

There had been a dread of going near Batty Green during that smallpox summer, yet in July a party of Settle people had gone ahead with plans to visit the railway works. A young lady with a love of adventure, and despite fervent entreaties from her lady companions, clambered on to the footplate of a locomotive as it started its run for Blea Moor tunnel. Then, durably attired, the lady descended in succession the three shafts of the tunnel.

In 1872, the indomitable Job Hirst – still occupied in viaduct building – had the joy of organising a party for 150 workmen and friends in the Schoolroom at Batty Green to mark the twenty-first birthday of Walter Pickard Hirst, his son. After the tables were removed, Mr Price, the Batty Green postmaster, was unanimously voted to the chair, apologising for the absence, through another appointment, of Mr W H Ashwell, the contractor. Mr Hancock, the missionary, proposed Walter's health. There were hearty cheers. A month later, Job was dead, aged 57 years.

An account of his death has been related in the family by his daughter, Nancy Ellen Hirst, to her niece until the present day. Job Hirst had gone to Ingleton in a horse and trap to fetch the men's wages. It was an arduous journey in a snowstorm. On the return journey, he was set upon by thieves, who took the wages and his gold watch, leaving him unconscious by the side of the road.

He regained consciousness, saw his horse patiently standing with the trap and noticed something was glittering by a nearby stile. It was his gold watch, hanging by its chain in the bushes. Job collected it, painstakingly climbed into the trap – and again lost consciousness. Meanwhile, Mary his wife, fretful because Job was late, waited up for him. In the late evening, she heard the sound of an approaching horse. It marked the return of Job's outfit. The horse had brought him home and he was lying on the floor of his trap. Job revived and was given a glass of port but in the morning Mary found him dead beside her. The doctor concluded he had died of an apoplectic fit – and the port was the worst thing he could have taken.

The grave of Job Hirst, who supervised the building of Ribblehead viaduct.

Job was buried at Chapel-le-Dale on December 11. The officiating clergyman was the Rev E Smith. The sub-contractor was held in such regard that a handsome bench-type tombstone, with a cross at one end, was positioned over the grave. It had a prime site, to the right of the path, immediately beyond the lych-gate. His sons Walter and Charles Henry supervised the completion of the viaduct. Mary Hirst went to live with her son Joshua at Woodseat, outside Sheffield. She died in 1883, aged 58, and would have been buried beside her husband – if a snowstorm had not prevented the trip.

When the Construction Committee met on the last day of 1872, Mr Ellis reported that, accompanied by the chairman, he had visited all the works on the Settle and Carlisle railway and found the progress made during the past four months deficient on all three contracts. Slow progress was attributed to excessive rainfall extending over the whole period and the difficulty in obtaining labour. He added: "The progress of the works in the hands of the company [Contract No 1] has been more rapid, but the cost has been much beyond the prices of the original contract." [This may explain why the company was more willing than previously to increase payment to the other contractors].

Ellis requested that particular works of a type likely to require the longest time for completion should be reported on monthly by Crossley. Among the "instances" were Blea Moor Tunnel and Ribblehead viaduct.

Chapter Five

Blea Moor Tunnel by candlelight – Law-breaking – The bad boys – A Sunday with the navvies.

Crossley's report on Contract No 1, dated May 30, 1870, had indicated that at Blea Moor the earth shifting was proceeding at about a third to two-fifths of the amount required for "on time completion". A tramway was being laid from the Ingleton road to the south face of the tunnel, a distance of two and one-eighth miles. One mile of track was in place. The machinery in situ at the north end of the tunnel included four locomotives, 440 wagons, three winding engines, three portable cranes and two steam cranes. By 1873, on Contract No 1, there were ten locomotives and eighteen portable and stationary engines. This Victorian workforce consisted of about 1,800 men.

One of the locomotives brought in by the Midland Railway when it took over Contract No 1 for building the southern portion of the Settle-Carlisle line. "Derby No 9" was photographed at Helwith Bridge.

A vertical steam engine possibly of the type used for the shafts on Blea Moor.

Reporting to the Construction Committee, Crossley mentioned a major complication at Blea Moor – a large cutting at the south end of the tunnel with $1\frac{1}{2}$:1 slopes (218,000 cubic yards). These slopes would require to be flattened. An enormous amount of earth shifting would be involved. To avoid this, it was contemplated extending the length of the tunnel by some 200 yards. Progress, as ever, depended on the recruitment of a sufficient number of men and making it worth while for them to remain.

The tramway laid to Blea Moor made clever use of the contours, although in places the gradient was as steep as 1 in 18. Locomotive drivers would be apt to cross-fingers for good luck prior to reaching a simple wooden structure which served as a bridge. It creaked ominously. A visitor in the summer of 1873 was impressed by the novel way in which a beck was being carried over the line. [It has since been referred to as an aqueduct.] The contemporary account mentioned "a watertight inverted stone course for Force-gill beck to run over the line."

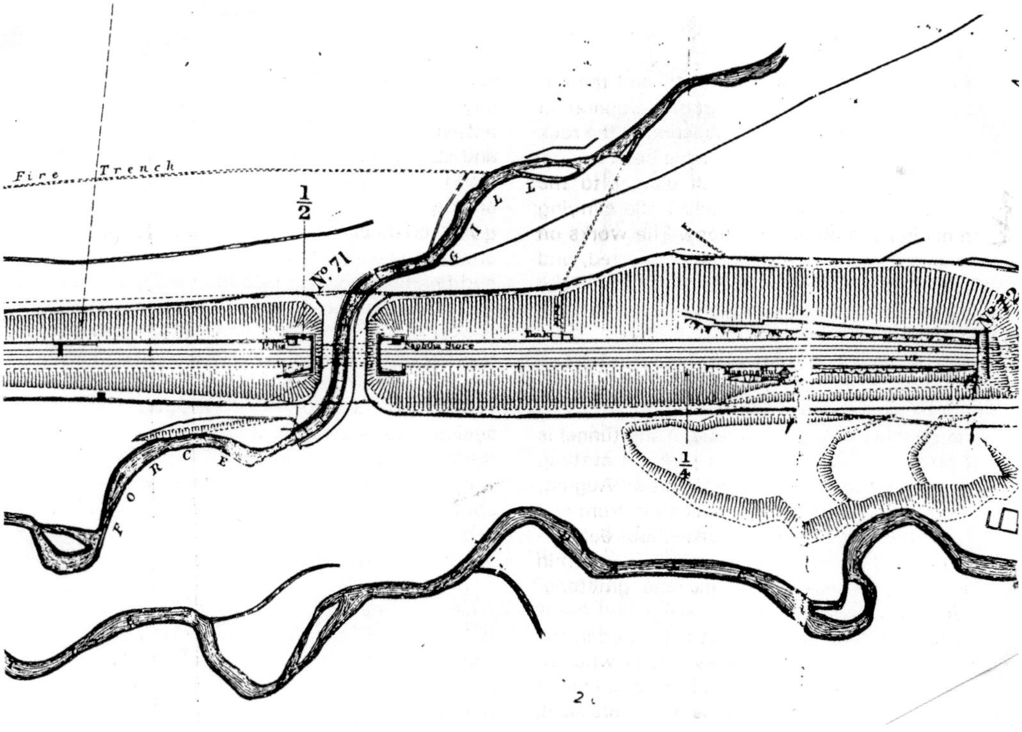

The Midland Railway's "Land Map" of the southern end of Blea Moor tunnel showing the aqueduct built to carry Force Gill Beck over the line.

The area to the north of Blea Moor was ravaged by a fierce storm in 1870. Thunder, lightning and torrents of rain fell from "dark and hanging clouds". Heavy blocks of limestone, torn from their beds, were carried over 100 yards by the rolling flood "and tossed upon heaps as if by magic."

Events in the tunnel were graphically described by a correspondent of the Westmorland Gazette: "The day was intensely hot up to about three o'clock, when all became nearly dark over the tunnel at Dent Head. Presently, one flash of lightning succeeded another, accompanied with loud thunder and, without a minute's warning, the water poured down as if from a water-spout for about two hours." Five miners were at work inside the tunnel and about 40 yards from its mouth. Before they were aware of the magnitude of the storm, water gushed into the tunnel, almost filling it.

Three men escaped. Two of their fellow workmen were trapped. "As soon as assistance arrived, one young man, to whom great praise is due, swam up the tunnel where the water was about two feet from the roof, and found a poor fellow standing upon an elevation with only his nose and the top of his head out of water, and with his fingers in his ears to keep the water out of his head. The brave young man who found him, on seeing his situation, returned and got a raft of wood, and swimming up the tunnel again, pushed the raft before him and placed the poor fellow upon it more dead than alive, and brought him out. He then returned up the tunnel with his raft in search of the other miner, and diving down to the bottom of the water he found the poor fellow, but life had been gone for some time."

The young man had been at the works for only a fortnight. His body was sent to King's Cliff in Nottinghamshire to be interred. "A sorrowful widow and two little ones, by this sudden and unexpected catastrophe, are left to mourn over their irreparable loss. The loss to Mr Ashwell, the contractor, was considerable. Nearly all the timber and railway plant near the tunnel was swept away."

Walter, Job's son, keen to inspect the work on Blea Moor Tunnel, about which he had been told, entrained to Tunnel Huts, at its southern end, beyond the shanties of Jericho and Jerusalem, from where, once a week, a market train operated. Womenfolk from high-lying shanties clambered into wagons drawn by a small steam locomotive that left Tunnel Huts at 2 p.m. The passengers were asked, for their own safety, to sit in the bottom of the wagons. So they were borne to the shops and services of Batty Green.

Walter's truck was in its workaday state. On his way to Blea Moor, he watched navvies clearing land for a cutting. Their "navvy wear" consisted of moleskin breeks, canvas shirt, velveteen coat and hobnail boots. There had been a slip of earth containing an estimated 20,000 cubic yards. The entrance to the south-end of the tunnel was now barred by a stout piece of rock that would soon be shifted. Then, it was said, one might go from one end of the tunnel to the other without descending any of the seven shafts that were excavated. Three shafts would be retained for ventilation.

Blea Moor tunnel was made to curve slightly for about 350 yards at the southern end. The effect of being able to look right through the tunnel was lost but, as related, a railway which, on paper, was heading for Whernside, must on plans and in reality curve towards Blea Moor. Seven stationary steam engines were in use, two for winding materials up the incline planes from each end, the rest for pumping and winding the excavations up the shafts. Until the ends joined up, the shafts were used to lower bricks and mortar for work in the tunnel.

Walter used No 1 shaft, which would be retained for ventilation. A 12-inch winding engine, which was drawing up tubs of debris from the tunnel, was made available for Walter's descent to the subterranean workplace of no less than 300 miners, bricklayers and labourers. The work was being pushed forward with considerable force. It was assessed that the bricklayers with their servers laid about 35,000 bricks in three days. Each week, about 70,000 bricks were positioned.

A 16-inch engine pumped the water and blew air to the men at the bottom. Walter was told that No 2 shaft, also permanent and sunk for 127-ft to foundation level, was now lined throughout with brickwork. The water met with varied from 80 to 100 gallons per minute. The available engine power had the capacity to raise 450 to 500 gallons per minute, so all was well.

No 3 shaft, at the Denthead side of the hill, had been sunk at an earlier stage. Air was supplied to the men at the face of the heading by means of a long column of water in a wrought-iron pipe, which had its outlet through a rose fixed on the tip. The column of water had a pressure of 120 lb per square inch. Consequently, the rush of water drove the air up the pipe 11 inch by 9 inch to the face of the heading – a force of air was so strong it was said to be able to blow out a candle at a range of two or three yards.

Walter stopped beside a clattering steam engine. The winchman, having fed it with cobs of coal, recalled when donkeys carried coal in sacks. Walter's winch descent to the heart of the Moor delivered him to a tunnel partly obscured by wraiths of smoke from explosives. More blasting took place. Walter felt compression on his ear drums.

He was shown a stick of dynamite. It was pinkish and by candlelight resembled boiled lobster! Walter heard it was expensive, costing £200 a ton. A major factor in the price was transportation by road from Carlisle and Newcastle. Miners had an almost cheerful disregard for safety measures connected with dynamite. Unexploded dynamite was left in holes in the rocks when it should have been removed in case it was struck by a driller who was unaware of its presence.

In May, 1874, John Roberts and Caleb James (the latter known as Birmingham Bill) were drilling when old dynamite exploded. Bill died soon afterwards. Roberts lost an eye and the sight in the other eye was greatly impaired. Henry Wright, working a night shift that November, was

Thunder in the mountains! A Blea Moor miner using a novel form of explosive called dynamite.

killed by an explosion of dynamite from an old hole in rock. Someone had broken the rule of covering such a hole with clay as a warning to others. In the explosion, Henry's arms were broken and his body seriously injured. At Batty Green hospital, he was attended by the company's doctor but died; he was 24 years of age. The funeral cortege was on a now familiar route to the churchyard in Chapel-le-Dale.

At about 11-00 a.m on the morning of 5 February, 1875, a 28-year-old miner named John Thompson was alone and in the act of drying some dynamite – a foolhardy action and contrary to orders. An explosion occurred. Two men went to the spot and found the young miner's body dreadfully mangled and lifeless. The fragments were sorrowfully gathered up and conveyed to the hospital at Batty Green. At an inquest held at the Welcome Home, a jury reached the verdict of accidental death. Thompson was buried at Chapel-le-Dale on the day the inquest took place.

Tallow candles, the only means of illumination, cost the company £50 a month. A visitor mentioned the "dimly burning candles, uncouth-looking wagons standing on the rails or moving to and fro, men at the facings, some above and some below, with their numerous lights like twinkling stars in a hazy night, the noisy of the twirling drills beneath the terrible force of big hammers being used by stalwart men..." The workforce had attuned themselves to the distinctive properties of solid rock – to black limestone, gritstone and the few beds of slate. Horses in the tunnel were sleek in their skin and in fine condition, their heads bedecked with ribbons by their proud drivers.

Henry Cartwright, a miner aged about 23 years of age, died in the weak light of candles when he was hit by a piece of displaced rock. He was working underneath a travelling stage. The rock had fallen from near the top of the tunnel. It was a large stone – 3-ft 6 in by 2-ft – and it lay on his loins. The coroner returned a verdict of accidental death.

A correspondent of the Lancaster Guardian vividly summed up what he had observed on his journey into the underworld: "No person can walk in the tunnel for an hour or more and listen to the thundering reports and reverberations of blasting, see the miners wielding with terrible force their sledge-hammers when drilling the hard rock, and breathe the thick smoke of the exploded dynamite, without feeling sympathy for those employed in such mining operations, and of seeing what a privilege it is to travel by rail at the rate of a penny a mile."

When the tunnelling was constricted, men lay down, now and again, to gulp in the lower stratum of air. An inspector said that one man was so overcome by obnoxious fumes he had to be brought down from the heading and given time to get his breath. A miner drilled the hard rock with hammer and 'jumper', this being a sharp pointed metal bar used to drill holes for explosives. He moved the jumper slightly between blows so that the cutting edge changed continually.

Black damp had been met with in the heading. Also what was described as an explosive stone. The men reckoned that compressed air in the hill forced the stone outwards when it had been partly excavated. Some of the sidewalls needed to be reinforced with brick, varying in thickness from 1-ft 6 inches to 3-ft. Each week about 70,000 bricks were laid. Two bricklayers, with attendant labourers, operated on each side of the tunnel and in support were two mortar-carriers.

Relays of tunnellers worked steadily from Sunday night at ten until Saturday night at the same time, with a change of teams at 6 a.m. and 6 p.m. Mining was repetitive work – hand-drilling, filling the holes with gun-cotton or gunpowder, igniting by means of a time-fuse then waiting for the big bang. The debris was cleared away either up the shafts in baskets or in wagons at the open end, the brick lining following as soon as possible. About 16 yards of tunnel were completed in a week.

Material from the ends of the tunnel was removed by horse-drawn trolley. James Sherman, a horse and cart driver working at the north end of the tunnel, had an ankle crushed when he tripped and the wheel of a wagon passed over it. James had neglected to keep the tunnel lighted. The accident was not considered serious but he was weakened through a loss of blood while being moved in an open cart over several miles of rough track to his lodgings at Batty Green. Blood began to trickle from the cart, yet Sherman refused medical aid. He bled to death.

Pay-day at Batty Green, with navvies lining up outside the "Contractor's Hotel".

Drawing of the "Contractor's Hotel", from Williams' history of the Midland Railway.

How the men were paid – and how forgery of sub-tickets met with the utmost severity of the law – was revealed during a case at Ingleton Court in May, 1874, when the appropriately-named John Money, a miner in Blea Moor Tunnel, was brought before the Ingleton magistrates on the charge of tampering with a sub-ticket with the intent of defrauding the Midland.

James Bennett, timekeeper at the tunnel, said the prisoner had been working on his shift for about six weeks. Saturday, 25th of the month, was pay day, the men being paid up to Wednesday night. The subsequent three days were carried on to the next fortnight's account. On the afternoon of the previous day, Money had applied for a sub-ticket to the amount of 10s, which was given to him in the tunnel on Saturday morning. The ticket was produced in court. Joseph Thomas Jones, assistant agent to the Midland company, said that part of his work was to pay the tunnel workmen. On Saturday, between 10 and 10-30 a.m, Money had come to him for pay. He was paid up to Wednesday night.

After receiving his pay, he presented his sub-ticket for cash and the amount written upon it. The 10s had been made into 40s. He was given the 10s but was informed that as he had tampered with the ticket he would prosecute him. Money said: "I do not care; the ticket has never been out of my hands."

PC Cameron had taken Money into custody on the charge of attempting to defraud the Midland company. One Michael Nolan, charged with a similar offence but with a smaller amount, had added 10d to his sub-ticket of 12s. For the attempt to defraud the railway company in the first instance of 30s and of 10d in the second case, the bench decided to commit the two prisoners to the next assizes to be held at Leeds.

When the breakthrough occurred, the temperature of the headings fell from 80 degrees to 57 degrees. The headings met within three inches, a distance of 924 yards having been driven from the two ends. A correspondent of Wildman's Household Almanack who visited the tunnel in 1875, and found it was nearing completion, was told it would be finished by February lst, next year. "A small amount of brick lining remains to be done, together with cleaning up and putting in a central drain to carry away the water that finds itself into the tunnel...A shaft 40-ft in diameter is about to be built at the point where the curve commences, for ventilation and light."

At the north end of the tunnel the face of masonry had been built "and a large stone with the date 1871 cut on it". The masonry was fine and well worthy of inspection. In the autumn of 1875, 'Rambler', a regular correspondent of the Lancaster Guardian, had the much-prized experience of being on a locomotive that entered the tunnel at the north end. "When about half-way through a fog signal made the engine driver greatly diminish his speed. Shortly we came to a number of workmen whose dimly burning candles made the deep excavation look all the more gloomy. The sounds of the shrill whistle of the engine were so loud and discordant that one was glad to weaken the sensation by putting one's fingers in the ears."

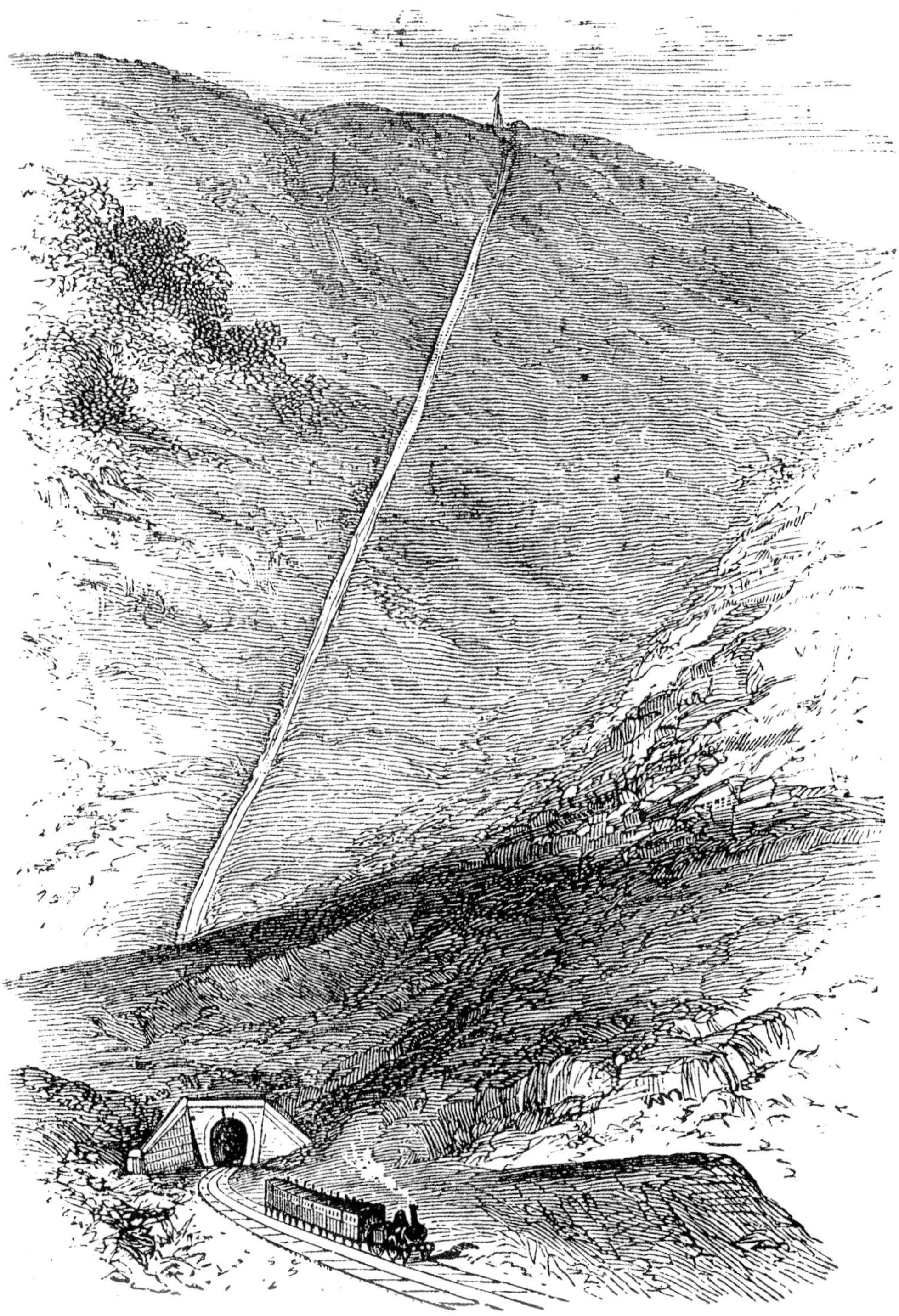

The north portal of Blea Moor tunnel. This drawing accompanies F S Williams' graphic account of his journey through the tunnel before emerging into "the sweet bright light of heaven".

F S Williams, Midland historian, writing in 1876, described a visit to the tunnel from the south. "We can now see through the 'spectacles' of the powerful little engine which is drawing us, that we are approaching the mouth of what may perhaps be more strictly called the 'covered way' that leads to the famous Blea Moor Tunnel...We are now in the tunnel. Nothing is to be seen but the lamp, which our engineer has just lit, dangling from the roof, and throwing its bull's-eye light on the tunnel wall. Nothing is heard but the roar of our puffing snorting little engine, and the hollow reverberation of the mighty cavern.

"Onward we go, beneath a mountain, which rises yet 500-ft above our heads, when suddenly some sharp shrill whistles are sounded, the speed is slackened, and we find ourselves slowly moving among groups of scores of men with flickering lights and candles stuck on end on the projecting crags of the rocky tunnel sides. For a moment we pause. 'What's up?' shouts a deep voice; and some answer, inarticulate to us, is returned.

"The steam is turned on; again we move forward into the thick black night; other whistles follow; other lights glimmer and gleam; another group of workmen is passed, looking, by the red light of their fire, a picture fit for Rembrandt; and at last, not unwillingly, we emerge into the sweet bright light of heaven."

Miners who showed considerable bravery underground were inclined to absorb too much drink during their leisure hours. The unenviable task of maintaining law and order in the hutments was sustained by a small police force. When Contract No 1 was negotiated in 1869, the successful applicant had to provide the necessary police as required by the local magistrates. Supt William Exton and Sergeant William Clapham were stationed at Ingleton. Batty Green was patrolled by PC Archie Cameron. Death was common enough for T P Brown, deputy coroner, to be kept busy questioning the survivors.

The most clannish section consisted of so-called Liverpool Irishmen, who had worked on the Mersey docks. Some English labourers harboured such a deep hatred of the Irish that on three occasions one Thomas Brown threatened to burn down an Irishman's hut, as testified in a case at the West Riding courthouse, Ingleton, where the duty magistrates were J Farrer, Esq., and the Rev R Denny. Elizabeth Murphy, wife of the Irishman, recalled that the offensive words were: "Come out of that, or we will fetch you out. If you are not out by four o'clock tomorrow, we will bring your things out and burn the bloody hut down."

The defendant denied the charge and told the Bench he was not present at the hut mentioned. Nonetheless, he was bound over to keep the peace for six months in two sureties of £50 each and himself in £100. On the tunnel project, the English and Irish worked amicably, racial differences being forgotten in the face of common dangers in the dark, dank world of shafts and headings.

A popular alternative name to Demon Drink was John Barleycorn. It was written that "the navvies appear, when maddened by drink, to set all law and all law officers at defiance, so that when alcohol and passion rage it becomes dangerous for anyone to interfere". The ale-can was held responsible for most of the crime, beer being retailed at sixpence a quart. One sorrowful comment was: "Drink has been a gigantic hindrance." In 1871, Mr Ashwell, contractor, attempted to combat the drink menace by confiscating six barrels of beer, which were then stove in. Interference with the drink traffic was organised by the Settle Temperance Society. Some of its members visited the hutments in the hope of getting topers to sign the pledge (that they would restrain from drink in its alcohol form).

John Barwise, an excise officer, inquire into illicit drinking among the navvies and presented evidence about it at the courts. He pressed the Sedbergh Bench to impose a heavy penalty in a case where a man was accused of selling beer without a licence; this plea for severity was "on account of the quantity of excisable liquor which is illegally sold by the hut-keepers on the new line of railway." The fine was £2.

Inns were convenient venues for inquests. In 1870, an inquest was conducted at the house of John Garlick near Batty Wife Hole. On other occasions, the coroner was at the Railway Inn and Welcome Home at Batty Green, the last-named being presided over by James Mathers. He was described as "an innkeeper of Batty Green, Ingleton Fells." Alas, poor James. He would meet his end on a visit to Ingleton. Stopping near the Wheat Sheaf Hotel he removed the collar of his horse so he might give the animal some meal.

Before James could replace the collar, the horse bolted. He ran after it, was knocked down and his neck run over by a wheel of his conveyance. Death was instantaneous. So well regarded was James Mathers that a large headstone was reared at his grave in the Chapel-le-Dale churchyard. His wife took over the Welcome Home. She is also said to have organised a pawn-broking business. Most of the money she loaned to customers was almost immediately returned – as takings at the bar.

Peter Miles, a navvy who had been drinking at the Welcome Home, staggered forth and found the tramway was relatively dry. He decided to use it to sleep off his inebriated condition. On the next day, the luckless man was decapitated by the first train. The guard of an engine returning from Jericho told an inquest that when the engine was about 150 yards from Batty Green platform, a jerk was felt. He ordered the driver to stop the locomotive and found the body of Miles. The dead man was 30 years old and a native of Bootle.

The Railway was a particularly handy inn which, in course of time, would become the stone-built Station Inn. One of the hostelries stood at the roadside at Newby Head, having an appeal for those travelling from Ingleton to Hawes. Robert Lodge was classified by the census-takers as "licensed victualler & farmer of 40 acres of land." He had his drink problems, though not as extreme

Gearstones, on the old turnpike, with the former inn on the left`.

as Francis Yates, who was the licensee, with his daughter Alice, of Gearstones; he also farmed the attendant 55 acres.

There were few dull moments at Gearstones. It was here, in 1868, that the surveying party under the engineer Sharland found lodgings and stayed much longer than expected when snowfall inhibited movement for several days. At Gearstones in May, 1873, George Young, railway worker, under the influence of strong drink, tossed dynamite on to the fire, slightly injuring some customers, blowing into pieces the kettle in front of the fire, and damaging the building, though slightly. Fragments of the kettle were produced in evidence at a hearing at Ingleton Court House the following day.

The police and magistrates were kept busy with a wide range of law-breaking. The Rev Denny, vicar of Ingleton for 28 years until March, 1874, when he headed for a new home at Tatham rectory, joined fellow magistrates in committing naughty navvies to spells at the Wakefield House of Correction. Denny and J T Rice were duty magistrates in June, 1872, when Richard Rogers was apprehended for killing a grouse on the liberties of James Farrer, Esq.

On the 10th day of the month, the defendant was seen by Robert Staveley, the new gamekeeper on the Ingleton Fell preserve. Rogers was among the young grouse. He picked up a bird and it was found in his possession. He pleaded guilty and was find 20s and costs of 14s. As the money was not forthcoming, he was committed to gaol for one month. Staveley, gamekeeper, appeared in a case where John Jones, a youth, of Batty Green, was charged with doing damage to Mr J J Farrer to the amount of 2d. The lad had been trespassing on Farrer's moor, stooping occasionally as though looking for grouse eggs. He was fined 5s, with 11s costs, and the aforementioned tuppence for damage done to the herbage on the moor.

That year, Gamekeeper Staveley encountered James Simpson and Samuel Gilibrand, of Batty Green, who were supposedly looking for trout in Cam Beck, part of the Farrer estate. They were brought to Court on a day when one of the magistrates was – Mr Farrer. He naturally retired. Simpson, who was present, pleaded "not guilty", asserting that no fish were caught. The gamekeeper had approached them only four minutes after they reached the beck. Simpson was fined 1s and 7s.6d costs. Gilibrand, who did not appear, was fined 10s and 11s.6d costs.

Testimony given at the magistrates' court gave insight into aspects of railway life that might otherwise have been forgotten. Denny and J Teal, Esq., were on the Bench when Thomas Jones, a railway labourer, commonly known as Welsh Knobby, was charged with robbing the shop window of John Clark Garlic, innkeeper and grocer at Batty Green. Fifteen items had been taken. P C Cameron produced some of them – an oil lamp and five pieces of scented soap, the value of which was 8s.

The case was involved, and adjourned, but not before it was revealed that drunken men who were locked out of their lodgings were inclined to make for the engine shed at the tunnel. Matthew Frost, for the defence, was an engine driver who had known the prisoner from sight since Monday (on the night of which the alleged burglary took place). Said Frost: "He came into the engine shed at the tunnel a little before 12 o'clock on Monday night. He was with another man and they were drunk and linked arm in arm to hold each other up. He stopped in the shed until four o'clock next morning."

Another curious case was related to Daniel Mellor Edson, a general dealer of fish, and Matthew Hall, his boy. They were at the shanty called Jericho when (it was alleged) Thomas White, a railway labourer, stole a mackerel and assaulted the two visitors. The proferred evidence was that while the boy was plying his trade outside a hut, White took a mackerel out of his basket and went into the hut, followed by the boy, who asked him to return the fish. Instead, he beat the lad with a pick shaft. Edson, approaching White to get the mackerel, was savagely beaten on the side of the head and face with the self-same pick shaft.

Luckily, two policemen who were on duty not far away apprehended White and had him locked-up at Ingleton. Brought before the magistrates, he pleaded guilty to the charges. For stealing the mackerel, he was sent to prison for two months, plus a month's imprisonment for each assault. Many offenders served their time in the Wakefield House of Correction.

The police used the national telegraph system. Edward Town, a sub-contractor, had a wife and family at Swansea. He bigamously married a daleswoman at Horton-in-Ribblesdale church and was apprehended by P C Goodison, who had received a telegraph message from Swansea, via Settle. Supt Exton, of Ingleton, had sent a message to the constable at Gearstones. A telegraph was sent to Swansea stating that Edward Town had been apprehended. Back, by telegram, came instructions that he should be taken to Lancaster, "where Mr Supt Allison will be waiting."

One Sunday morning, a navvy named John Atkins, better known as Policeman Jack, fought William Williams (alias Nobby Scandalous) on the road from Dent Head to Ingleton. Williams died. At the inquest it was stated that the fight lasted fifteen minutes; the two men had been sober, fought with their fists and did not kick. Thomas Wright testified that the men appeared to be equally matched and at the fourth round they both fell. Williams, by now speechless, died five minutes later. Atkins, scared, took to the hill in the direction of Newby Head, by way of Batty Green to Ingleton.

The Dent Head policeman traced Atkins to Thornton-in-Lonsdale, where – in classic phraseology – all traces of him were lost. The superintendent and his officers did all they could, in the absence of the telegraph and railway locomotion, to send or convey messages to other stations so that the whereabouts of the runaway might be discovered. The cause of death, according to Dr Griffiths, who carried out the post mortem examination, was the infusion of blood on the brain. It might have been caused by a bruise on the scalp. The jury returned a verdict of manslaughter. Atkins was committed to take his trial at the next assizes.

Many of the Batty Greeners were sports-mad. If, within a few miles of the line, there were organised sports, railway work – locomotives, tunnels, bridges, brickworks – were vacated. The navvy loved wrestling, running and leaping – after he had a spell of hard drinking.

To combat boredom and elevate the mind, a reading room was opened, the periodicals being supplied free of charge by the oft-mentioned Burgoyne and Cocks. Sunday was theoretically a rest day. A correspondent of the Lancaster Guardian visited Blea Moor in August, 1872, and gave a detailed account of "A Sunday with the Navvies".

He commented on how little interest Christian ministers and members of their churches took in the moral and spiritual welfare of those railway workers and their familes, "who for the public good are in a great measure cut off from the ameliorating and Christianising influence of society. Many of those men have not entered a place of worship for years, and few of them have ever been kindly spoken to about their eternal welfare."

The newspaper correspondent noted that the Midland had a railway missionary on the spot but he could not witness effectually on the whole length of No 1 Contract. "On a Sabbath-day his labours are almost confined to Batty Green, so that Sebastopol, Jericho, Jerusalem, Tunnel Huts, &c, where the inhabitants, children and adults are numerous, are entirely neglected. If any class of men have a right to say 'No man cares for my soul' it is those men who make our great public iron highways."

If the clergy and ministers in the neighbourhood of the line would give a Sunday now and then, and in their mission tours distribute a few narrative tracts, who could tell how useful might be the results? "No one need fear engaging in this work if he has a loving heart, for kind words uttered with brotherly feeling will always win the attention and respect of railway labourers, whether drunk or sober."

The writer, who was a Wesleyan local preacher, and Mr Hancock, the railway missionary, had arranged to hold open-air services on Blea Moor at the different hut villages on Sunday, the 4th. They "hailed with more than common joy the beautiful sunny morning" and saw "at one sweeping view Ingleborough, Whernside, Penyghent, Fountains Fell, Pendle Hill with other hills too numerous to mention." The two men hastened to Denthead, which had a mission-house supported by Wesleyans from Dent and Sedbergh, who conducted services on Sunday afternoon. Several railway workers held a Sunday School.

Mr Ashwell, the contractor, had made a horse-drawn trap to convey them to their first meeting place. "After we commenced with singing, the workmen gathered round, and listened to the various discourses with great attention...Many of the hearers were in their shirt sleeves, some smoking, one holding a cat and another a dog. Many of those men are very fond of animals and consequently set their affections on either birds, fowls, dogs, cats, &c....Though Saturday night was pay-night, it was pleasant to see that none of them was under the influence of drink."

At the close of the service, there was food to meet the necessities of locals and visitors. After dinner, the missionaries started for Jericho, on the south side of Blea Moor. "We had to leave the highway and climb the steep tramway up the mountain. On the top of Blea Moor, where there are a few huts, we sang a portion of a hymn, after which the missionary spoke a few friendly words to some who stood at their doors or looked out of their windows."

On the way down the hill they met a tradesman with his well-filled pack on his back. "We spoke to him about plying his trade on the Sabbath-day. He charged us in return with making profit by our Sunday labour, but fortunately he was under a mistake. Some will be surprised when we state that drapers, tea dealers, shoe merchants, clock and watch dressers, &c go from house to house and from railway village to railway village with their merchandise on the Sabbath-day as on other days."

At the Tunnel Huts, there was a good deal of drinking and many of the navvies were under the influence of drink. "We distributed a few tracts and spoke a few friendly words to the men, who were very civil. If a navvy should chance to show a little rudeness, he would soon be checked by his mates. There is a day school here and it is said to be well attended. No-one can pass over these railway works without remarking on the great number of children."

At variance with Biblical geography, they left Jerusalem and descended to Jericho. "Many of the men were under the influence of drink but they treated us with respect. A number of men were playing at pitch and toss, but as soon as we began singing they ceased and came and listened very attentively. We soon had a pretty large gathering..." Seventy, indeed. A young man was noisily drunk but "he had no ill in him. Many of the men checked him again and again for his talking propensity."

When one of the missionaries mentioned prison life, a navvy was heard to say: "I've just come from a month of it." Another remarked of the mission meeting; "It was the happiest hour I've spent for three years." Like Dent, there was no lack of food. "It was quite amusing to see how some of those men who had just begun to feel the hilarious effects of drink came and took hold of our hymn-books and tried to catch the tune. Many a voice said at the conclusion: 'Come again.'

"After tea, we travelled to Sebastopol and Belgravia. After singing through Belgravia, we turned our feet to Sebastopol. As so many people were attracted by our song, the missionary and another man spoke a few friendly words to the listening crowd about their spiritual welfare. The people in the streets of Batty Green were remarkably good and orderly, contrasting with what they were on a previous occasion.

"On that evening, a drunken man ran hither and thither, big boys pelting him with mud, while numbers of laughing spectators were looking on. The poor man's face was covered with dirt and there was no telling what might have been the end of their fun had not a stranger checked them. Shortly after this scene, two men were apprehended for a house robbery and carried away by the police to the Ingleton lock-up. Today there was far more of the quiet of the Sabbath than the writer had ever witnessed on the Blea Moor railway works. None of the locomotives, the tunnel engines nor any of the men were at work."

The railway building would not last for ever. In the summer of 1873, about a hundred men were employed on the big viaduct and, as the weather had been for some time remarkably fine, the works under the management of Messrs Charles and Walter Hirst had made great progress. Blea Moor tunnel was "in a great state of forwardness".

A journalist considered it advisable to take food when visiting the uplands. "Breakfasting at Gearstones Inn before seven o' clock in the morning made one ready for one's tea between two and three o'clock in the afternoon, Should anyone who is given to eating and drinking decide to travel the whole length of the new line, it will be well for him to furnish himself with some provision, for the country is so sparse of inhabitants, and especially inns, that when he gets one meal he cannot tell where he will get the next."

The Settle and Carlisle extension of the Midland Railway was opened for goods traffic in August, 1875. The Midland directors recommended a dividend on ordinary stock for the half-year at the rate of 6 per cent per annum. By the autumn of that year, many of the huts on Batty Green had been removed. A goodly number of workers and their families had drifted away. Those who remained were kept busy. Crime-wise, the scene was calm. PC Walker, the only policeman, lived at Thornton-in-Lonsdale and maintained peace in a beat of more than ten miles.

The Settle-Carlisle line was opened, without an official ceremony, in May, 1876. The first passenger train left Skipton at 7-15 am. Settle was the first stopping place and, to quote the tireless correspondent of the Lancaster Guardian, "the explosion of fog signals as the train entered the new station was immediately followed by loud and hearty cheers from a crowd which had assembled on the platform."

He reported that the first express train from Edinburgh and the North consisted of eight vehicles, two Pullman cars, three of the new long carriages on the bogie principle, and three composite brake carriages. About Kirkby Stephen, "the hills were clothed in a white mantle of snow, which added to the beauty of the prospect." The train reached Skipton almost to a minute of the appointed time.

On to Settle, which presented a strange and confused picture. The construction of the station was almost finished. A sale of surplus material from the construction days was imminent. The lots would include two conspicuous items from Batty Green, the four-wheeled covered wagon-type ambulance and the bog-cart. The strange appearance of the cart would evoke much comment from visitors.

An explanation was offered to the journalist by someone who used it: "We used to fill it with victuals or clothes or bricks, to send the men at work on the line, across bogs where no wheels could go...I've seen three horses in a row pulling at that concern over the moss till they sank to their middle and had to be drawn out one at a time by their necks to save their lives."

The train had arrived at Settle during the dinner hour when "a strange silence prevailed throughout the works." Navvies were in repose on "piled-up baulks of timber". The men were "in various and grotesque attitudes, apparently sleeping as composedly and certain snoring as satisfactorily as any alderman would hope to do in his feather bed."

The dinner hour over, a busy tribe of masons resumed their chip-chipping of rough stones into shape. The carpenters were fitting their timbers together and cattle were driven into trucks for the dinners of the colony at Batty Wife Hole up the line. The locomotive on which the first-day visitors were travelling, drew up with full steam alongside the platform. Mr Ferguson, the company's engineer, was ready to start.

The passengers were ready also and in a minute the engine and its rake of carriages was puffing and snorting its way up the 1 in 100 gradient that extended for 14 miles to Ribblehead viaduct and the great Blea Moor tunnel.

1875
MR
MR

Chapter Six

Harry Cox goes under the arches and descends a shaft on Blea Moor – A walk through the Tunnel – Jack Towler and the 1947 snowstorm – Dawson family life at the trackside – When the Scots express left the rails.

Ribblehead viaduct was completed by 1875, an event marked by the setting of a large stone bearing the date 1875 at the centre of the parapet. The embankments on each side, having been joined up to the masonry, were sown with a ryegrass mix. It was an astonishing feat of engineering. The arches of 45-ft span were judged to have dropped a quarter of an inch when the supports were removed.

The Settle-Carlisle line opened for freight traffic in August 1875 with the first passenger trains starting in springtime 1876. In fact, J Pilgrim had driven the locomotive Diamond – the first engine to pass over Ribblehead viaduct – on Sunday, September 6, 1874. It carried five passengers, a stoker and a guard. The first passenger train was run as an experimental trip. One of Mr Kirtley's green-painted locomotives hauled a Pullman drawing room and sleeping cars from Skipton to Carlisle in two hours five minutes, at an average speed of 43 miles an hour.

1875 – the year when construction of the Settle-Carlisle railway was finally completed. The date is inscribed on both the south portal of Blea Moor tunnel and the centre of the parapet on Ribblehead viaduct, seen here with Tony Freschini who supervised the extensive restoration work in the 1980s.

Matthew Kirtley did not live to see his creation storm the Long Drag, for which they had been designed. He died at his office in 1873. Compared with the locomotives of later years, the Kirtleys were slight, their cabs limited in size. Yet their devoted crews, though exposed to wind and weather, inspired them to great efforts.

The cost of the line was £3.6 million – 50 per cent above the estimate. It was an enormous sum for Victorian days. The Settle-Carlisle had taken considerably longer to build than was planned. Yet a lucrative goods service would soon develop, with large numbers of cattle and sheep being conveyed from Scotland to the English marts.

Thousands of pounds worth of equipment from Contract 1 were auctioned off at Settle during the week beginning 24 May 1876. A special train from Leeds carried 200 intending purchasers to view the 1,200 lots spread for nearly a mile along the trackside at the new Settle station. F S Williams, historian, touring the line at about this time, saw Mr Ashwell's old caravan (nick-named the Contractor's Hotel), also the curious bog cart and the ambulance that was a modification of a covered wagon.

Three hundred lots were sold on the first day of sale. Buyers had come from as far off as Birmingham, Derby and Liverpool. Up for sale were various locomotives, also boilers, 70 wagons, 400,000 bricks, nearly 400 tons of contractors' rails, over 100 tons of scrap iron and 800 tons of firewood.

On the following day, the long-lasting dispute between the Midland and the Settle Highway Board was concluded. The railway company paid £100 towards the cost of repairing the road between Ingleton and Batty Green. By 1874, the number of residents of the hutments of Ribblehead was in rapid decline. Local residents feared that they would face increases in the rates. The combined rateable value of huts being removed was £600.

The Settle-Carlisle line was now under care and maintenance. The men engaged in viaduct work were given winter employment in the mile and a half long Blea Moor tunnel. It was a time for journalists to eulogise about the new railway. The Lancaster Guardian, which had given the most comprehensive reports of the progress of the line from its inception, observed that "the country through which the line passes is amongst the wildest and most romantic in England. It is a continued succession of high hills with intervening valleys, so that the line is alternately carried over viaducts, or through cuttings, or under hills hundreds of feet in height."

The Westmorland Gazette praised the new line but thought sadly that "the traveller...will miss some of its greatest beauties by his inability to see the bridges and viaducts on which it is carried." Among the structures mentioned was "a viaduct of 24 arches spanning the Ingleton valley", the Artengill viaduct of 11 arches and the Smardale viaduct. "Nearly all of these are remarkable for their great height; and although they are extremely simple in design, the tapering upwards of their lofty piers adds a a very pleasing elegance to their simplicity."

Readers were informed that the permanent way was laid throughout with 82lb steel rails and was adapted for heavy traffic and high speed. It was fitted with block signalling apparatus and interlocking points and levers. The wires to the distant signal were connected with an ingenious compensating apparatus that took up any slackness due to stretching or expansion and kept them always taut.

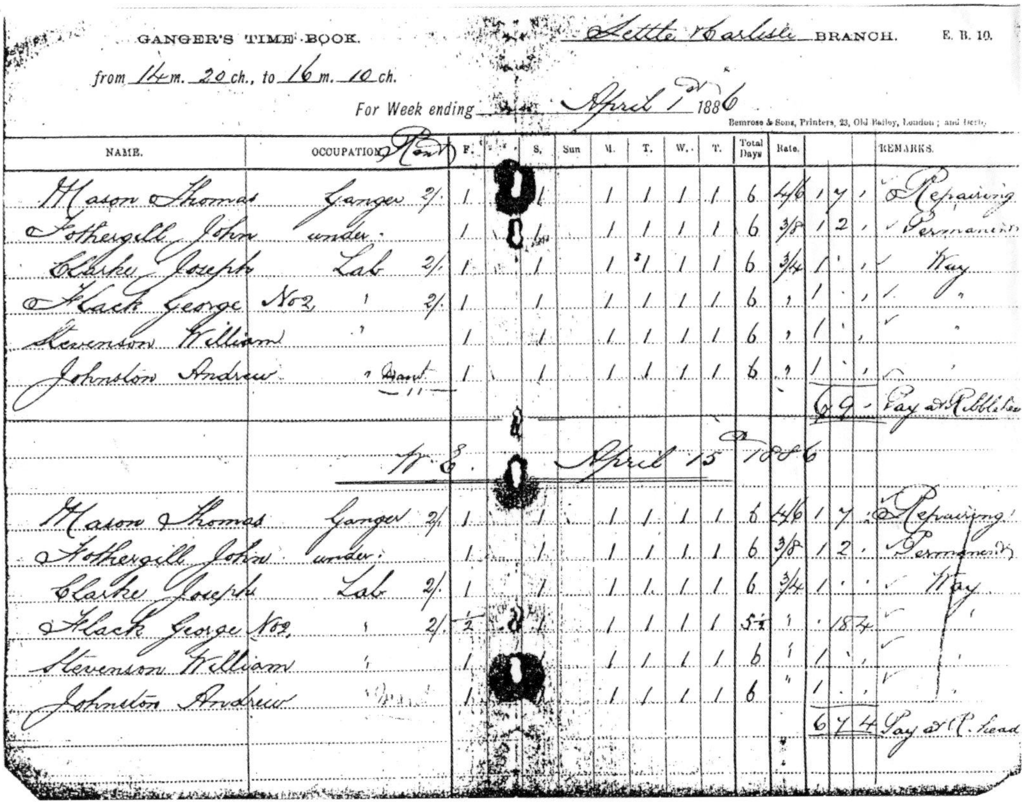

GANGER'S TIME BOOK. Settle & Carlisle BRANCH. E. B. 10.

from 14 m. 20 ch., to 16 m. 10 ch.

For Week ending April 1st 1886

Bemrose & Sons, Printers, 23, Old Bailey, London; and Derby.

NAME.	OCCUPATION.		F.	S.	S.	Sun	M.	T.	W.	T.	Total Days	Rate.				REMARKS.
Mason Thomas	Ganger	2/.	1		1		1	1	1	1	6	4/6	1	7	–	Repairing
Fothergill John	under		1		1		1	1	1	1	6	3/8	1	2	–	Permanent
Clarke Joseph	Lab	2/.	1		1		1	1	1	1	6	3/4	1	–	–	Way
Flack George No2	"	2/.	1		1		1	1	1	1	6	"	1	–	–	"
Stevenson William	"		1		1		1	1	1	1	6	"	1	–	–	"
Johnston Andrew	"		1		1		1	1	1	1	6	"	1	–	–	"
													6	9	–	Pay at Ribblehead
	W. E.				April 15						1886					
Mason Thomas	Ganger	2/.	1		1		1	1	1	1	6	4/6	1	7	–	Repairing
Fothergill John	under		1		1		1	1	1	1	6	3/8	1	2	–	Permanent
Clarke Joseph	Lab	2/.	1		1		1	1	1	1	6	3/4	1	–	–	Way
Flack George No2	"	2/.	½		1		1	1	1	1	5½	"		18	4	"
Stevenson William	"		1				1	1	1	1	6	"	1	–	–	"
Johnston Andrew	"		1				1	1	1	1	6	"	1	–	–	"
													6	7	4	Pay at R. head

Ganger's Time Book, dated April 1886.

Harry Cox, born at Workington in 1884 – only eight years after the opening of the Settle-Carlisle – became a railway employee in 1905. Harry was the newest member of the Extra Gang and thus was not guaranteed long-term employment. He might be made redundant at the end of the Gang's season of special work. This happened, but he rejoined the Gang next year and his services were subsequently retained.

Harry met Bill Hunt, a ganger in charge of the platelayers, and brother Jack, who ran the Extra Gang, which did the dirtiest work. Jack would say: "Go to our Bill at Horton." And the men would set off at 6 a.m, returning on Bonnyface, their nickname of the train from Hawes that picked them up at the end of their working day.

Jack Hunt was, according to Harry Cox, as ignorant a fellow as ever stepped in shoe leather. It was not altogether his fault; he had no schooling. Having to keep a record of the time worked by the men, he split each day into quarters. Apart from a personal name, not a word was written. If the whole day was worked, he would place a square against the man's name. If one of the quarters was not worked, there would be lines on three sides only.

The Extra Gang started work at 7 a.m but as the train from Skipton did not arrive until 8 a.m, ganger Jim Ion gave them odd jobs about Settle station for an hour. The same applied at the end of the week. The men had lodged away from Monday until Saturday; they arrived back at Settle at 11 a.m, with an hour to fill in before the end of work at noon. The Skipton men had to travel during that hour and were spared the extra duties. Said Harry: "All this for £1 a week!"

Railwaymen lived and breathed railways. It was known for Jack and Bill Hunt, when visiting the Crown at Horton in the evening, to draw on the floor the outline of points and crossings – the work to be done. Bill Hunt had a second man called Billy Morphet, who was a Methodist local preacher. Nonetheless, he was prevailed upon to read the news to the ganger each breakfast and dinnertimes. The news was entirely about horse-racing. Billy would read it with a poker-face, not having the slightest interest in racing. He would then have to go down to the bookmaker to place some bets for the ganger.

When the gang was working north of Blea Moor in August, the arrival of a grouse-shooting party to the lodge at Cowgill, head of the Dent valley, was observed. The building, a mini-mansion, was known as a lodge. At a discreet distance the railwaymen watched the arrival from Underley Hall, near Kirkby Lonsdale, of Lord Henry Bentinck, his posh friends, their wives, valets and maids. The party stayed for three or four days at a time. At grouse-shooting, the railwaymen stood a good chance of collecting an injured grouse or two that, having been injured by shot or hitting wires, had died, only to be overlooked by the shooting party.

Jackie Burton and his wife were caretakers at the shooting lodge. Said Harry: "The wife was boss. Jackie had to do everything she said. One day, two or three of us took Jackie to the Dub and got him drunk. We nearly had to carry him back. We didn't dare take him into the house. We just dumped him at the door, knocked and cleared off. Next day, he told us he'd woken up to find himself in the pig 'ole. His wife had put him there!"

One day, Harry and his pals were working on Denthead viaduct when three or four young women walked up the road. "We thought they were maids and started shouting at them – nothing objectionable, really, just arranging to meet them at the Cow Dub, a name for the Sportsman's Inn. It turned out they were lords' wives! They didn't report us or anything."

The railmen would visit the Cow Dub at night. "Valets gathered to play darts for pints of beer. The loser paid for a round. We got our ale for nothing. Thomas Burton was the landlord; his brother Dick was in the business. One of them looked after the inn; the other attended to the farm." There were other non-railway activities such as setting rabbit snares on the railway. "We were usually lucky and had a stew in the cabin towards the end of the week. It gave us a change of diet. Sometimes we took one or two rabbits home – though you could buy a rabbit in Settle for sevenpence!"

Harry added, reflectively: "I don't know if those were happy days or not. You had to do what you did. If you were out of work, you were out of work. There was no dole money or anything..." Harry joined the workers on Ribblehead viaduct and within Blea Moor tunnel.

At work, Harry wore an outfit that almost counted as a uniform – a coarse shirt and fustian trousers tied below the knee with a 'york', this being a leathern strip with a buckle. Some men used coarse string. A 'york' prevented the trouser ends from dragging in mud and yet allowed the knee and leg freedom of movement. Gangers tucked a flattened piece of wood, shaped rather like a knife blade, into one of the 'yorks'. Known as a 'minute stick', it was used to clean a shovel that had become clarted [clogged] with clayey-soil. The name 'minute' alluded to the time a man straightened his back after putting the stick to work.

Most men wore caps. Inspectors wore bowlers. A worker had big, heavy boots of the hob-nailed variety. (Arthur West had his boots hand-made at Dent at a guinea a pair). A clay pipe, purchased from a tobacconist, cost a penny. The bowl of the pipe was packed with black twist bought at thruppence an ounce. Harry smoked 4 oz of bacca a week. "You were somebody if you smoked using a wooden pipe. There was a lot of tobacco chewing – and spitting. A chap would come up to you when you'd produced some tobacco and say: 'Give us a chow'."

During "plugging and spiking" operations [track relaying] a nipper was set to work applying tar to the plugs and spikes. A stretch of track three-quarters of a mile long was dealt with at a time. Before the new track was laid, new sleepers arrived and were laid at the side of the railway.

Men working on piece rates who turned up two or three weeks before the large re-laying gang arrived were set to work, using a gauge, putting the iron "chairs" on the sleepers. They bored holes

These men walked from Skipton towards Carlisle, relaying the track in the late 1930s. Flat caps were almost universal.

with an augur, put on the "chair", placed a spike in one hole and a plug in the other. The nippers [new starters] then moved in to tar them.

On the appointed Sunday, up to 150 men would be mustered for track-laying. All the platelayers between Skipton and Hawes Junction were recruited. They took the old "road" out and put a new one in, using a well-established routine:

> *1. A gang knocked out the chocks.*
>
> *2. Two or three men tipped the rail.*
>
> *3. A gang followed, picking up the rail and carrying it to the side of the track.*
>
> *4. Another gang removed the old sleepers and stacked them.*
>
> *5. Gangs that completed their jobs came back and began installing the new track.*

The work took place in a regimented fashion. One lot fastened fishplates and joined the rails. The track had to be perfect before the line was re-opened. Even then, traffic was run over it at "caution", a flagman being in attendance and fog signals placed on the line to make drivers of trains know there was a new road. The line had to set [tighten itself] over the course of time.

When Harry and his pals were working on Ribblehead viaduct, they often faced strong winds from the west – winds that raced up Chapel-le-Dale and had their first obstruction when they strummed the arches of the viaduct. These arches seemed to suck the winds through and so, in turbulent weather, work on the viaduct had to stop. Small items – tools, etc – were either removed or firmly secured.

In modern times, scaffolding is in small lengths that are bolted together. Harry remembered when a crab [hand-operated winch] was used to draw up lengths of scaffolding a hundred feet long. A crab and the jack-roll worked on the same principle. "The crab was an ordinary winch and the jack-roll was a lot bigger. We'd assemble them, use them, then pull them into pieces and store them in the cabin."

Between 1905 and 1910, Harry Cox helped to re-brick the most northerly eight arches of the viaduct. At that time, platelayers were paid 19s a week, which was a shilling more than the wage of platelayers on the Morecambe railway line. Masons, who were considered to be more skilful, obtained £1 a week.

Re-bricking was spread over several summers. The first task was to fit cat-heads – full-length rails that were bent so as to fit under the railway line and then over a parapet. The turned-up piece at the end had a ring put round it. Piper Billy, a Scotsman who did blacksmith work, used a wagon coupling chain, fashioning it into a ring. To this blocks were attached. The rope extended from a "crab" set on the ground, passing through the blocks and back down to the ground, where it was attached by chain to heavy baulks of timber that had to be raised.

The next task was to erect scaffolding poles around the piers, ten to each pier. With a length of about 80-ft, the poles reached to just beyond the head of the piers. Two arches were attended to simultaneously. Harry's boss during this operation was Jackie Smith. The operation depended entirely on him, for there was no inspection to check that the scaffolding had been correctly erected.

Gorbels [masonry features] extended from the head of the piers, as they had done since the viaduct was made. They held the scaffolding erected in Victorian times when the arches were first bricked.

The "crab" enabled baulks of timber, each about forty feet long, to be raised and fitted from corbel to corbel, where they were wedged with iron 'pudlocks'. Four or five men were detailed to operate the "crab" and three men worked on the scaffolding. Two "catheads" were used, one on each side of the viaduct.

A baulk would be raised a foot or two and was then checked to ensure it was in perfect balance. On a signal, the winding continued, with two guy ropes in operation. These ropes were taken over by men high on the viaduct who were thereby able to guide a baulk into position. Then someone scampered across this temporary beam to unloose the chain and pulley. Another baulk was similarly handled.

When all the baulks were in positions, battens were raised and fitted between them to make a floor, which was about a day's job. Said Harry; "There was not a dance hall in Settle as big as that floor!" Every fifth batten was nailed down. In due course, three floors were in position, held firmly by struts and pillars.

The re-bricking of two arches having been completed, the timber was lowered to the ground with the "crabs" and moved by improvised tramway to the next arches. The bricks used were Staffordshire blues. At the end of the job, the scaffolding was loaded on to the ballast train, a task lasting two or three days, and taken through Blea Moor Tunnel for work on Denthead viaduct.

Harry recalled: "We had to lodge out in summer and were paid a shilling a night for our lodgings. We took a week's 'grub' with us in tin boxes and found accommodation in the area where we worked. I remember lodging with a platelayer at Dent and also at a farm at Colt Park during the time spent on re-bricking Ribblehead viaduct. (I heard of a 'rocking stone' in the woodland at Colt Park and was shown it by the farmer's son. It seems that in the railway-building days, navvies with crowbars tried to turn the stone. They never did. I saw the marks made by the crowbars)."

As Harry opened a "bait box" on a Monday night, he could see the food prepared for breakfast the following Saturday! "Monday's dinner and tea we carried in baskets. I would leave home with a basket in one hand and a stick in the other. That stick extended across my shoulder to the tin box containing the rest of the food. Mother made me four tatie pies. I remember they were in brown dishes. These pies were for dinner. I'd warm them up on the stove in the cabin. Other food included a pound of bacon."

During the time away from home, Harry might easily – and cheaply – buy fresh food. He quoted eggs at twenty-four for a shilling and butter at 7 1/2 d a lb. "At a farm near Denthead viaduct, I'd help to churn the butter on a Friday night. When I returned home on Saturday, my tin and basket were full of farm produce I was taking home. Wensleydale cheese. Rabbits I got at 7d each."

He remembered staying with an old ganger at Hawes Junction. The lodgings cost 2s.6d a week. The ganger's wife, when handed a coin at the week-end, would bite it to assure herself it was real. "Our lodgings were in one of the railway cottages. It had three bedrooms and there were six lodgers – two to a room."

Harry often wondered where the ganger and his wife slept. "One night we went down to

Looking out from the curved southern end of Blea Moor tunnel towards the aqueduct over the line.

Hawes for a night-out and missed the last train home. We had to walk back – six miles, following the track. When we got into the house we saw the old lady coming out of her dormitory – a cupboard under the stairs. She was covered with feathers. Presumably the ganger also slept there."

Blea Moor: this name stirs the heart of any railway enthusiast, in Settle or Surbiton, Carlisle or Cardiff. Mention it – and there comes to mind a rounded hill between the valleys of Ribble and Eden where the Midland engineers could not deviate in the face of a considerable natural obstruction. With Victorian verve, and precious little equipment beyond sticks of dynamite, shovels and the muscles of men, they drove a tunnel through the Moor at a cost of death, injury and the expenditure of £45 a yard. Human moles attended to a tunnel which, having a curve at the southern end, meant staring into blackness. There was no friendly circlet of light to be seen indicating the other end of the tunnel.

Harry recalled: "The summer was spent at Culgaith; we were re-bricking a shaft in Culgaith tunnel. In the evening, we'd go from village to village, from pub to pub. We were quite an attraction and did not have to pay for much beer, though it cost only tuppence a pint. You see, Billy Urquhart, a Scotsman, was leading the party playing his bagpipes; he was never without them. He would be followed by Alf Hocking, with a cornet, and Arthur West with a drum. The rest of us marched behind."

When Harry and his pals were working in Blea Moor Tunnel, they had to "watch out" when an express was passing through. "It was ten-to-one that a member of the catering staff would hurl out any unwanted food. We heard his food swish against the tunnel wall. It was against regulations, of course. One day we went into the tunnel with our naptha lamps and saw something glistening ahead. It turned out to be an enormous catfish. We carried it back to the cabin. It was hung up there for a day or two. We didn't sample it, for we wondered why, in the first place, the cook had thrown it away."

Blea Moor was wild – even in nice weather! A man driving a Derby 4 on the "down" line stopped at the water-crane near the signal box. With a goods train, a driver didn't gamble on the water-troughs at Garsdale. Up there, you were lucky if you got enough speed up to get half a tank. Filling the tank was therefore an "inside" job - up the goods line at Blea Moor. "One day, at the water column, the wind was so strong, a platelayer had to help me to hold the leather nozzle in the neck of the tank. We wrapped our arms around it, as though we were loving it."

Another night, a gale plucked several cars from transporter trucks at Ribblehead viaduct. A Garsdale ganger – one of the Harper family – was roused by Ted Ashton, the signalman, shouting up to say that some cars were lying in Blea Moor tunnel. There was a train in the "up" road and Ted had stopped it. The train gave the ganger a lift to Blea Moor and dropped him at the north end of the tunnel.

He walked through but saw no cars. He phoned from the end of the tunnel and the driver brought the train slowly through. The man walked on to Ribblehead viaduct. Six cars lay on their bonnets on the "up" road. It was a wild night. A freak guest of wind must have lifted them off. They were not normally fastened down.

Harry Cox said: "Blea Moor Tunnel was – wet! The Midland had allowed a worker a white blanket coat – which didn't stay white for long -–and thigh-length leggings. Naphtha lamps were used for illumination. If a worker felt devilish, he would accidentally knock one over, causing a blaze. If he felt even more devilish, he would toss something out of the darkness, knocking over one or two lamps. Then the tunnel seemed to be on fire." Some workers spurned lamps; they walked through the tunnel in darkness, using the four-foot, rapping a rail with a stick to keep on course.

Thirty yards in from the southern end was the Donkey Hole, blasted in solid rock. In Harry's time cement was stored here. About 50 yards inside the tunnel was a crevice between two rocks. "If we used a knife, we could extract some coal from the crevice. I suppose that at one time there was coal visible, but year after year a small amount was taken and gradually the crevice was deepened. It was quite a novelty to take some of this stuff home and tell friends we'd found the Blea Moor 'coal pit'."

Normally, a ganger tended a stretch two or three miles long. At the Blea Moor length, there was just Old Tom Marshall. "He cared for the tunnel and perhaps fifty yards on either side. In bad weather, he need not stray from the tunnel; in good weather, he might find a job to do in sunshine.

"Before the Great War, if the driver of a locomotive reported that water pouring from a ventilation shaft, some of the garlands [drainage channels] were blocked. The men had to de-block them. Over a couple of days, scaffolding was erected on the moor at the head of the shaft. A jack-roll [hand winch] holding a 120-yard stretch of wire rope was set up.

"Three men held a handle of the jack-roll and three men took hold of the other handle. The remaining man (often me!) had to go down the shaft to investigate and clean out the drainage system. I'd sit on a seat – it was just a piece of wood, fastened to the wire rope with a safety catch. A naptha lamp was hung on the seat. A man was stationed down in the tunnel; he was able to talk to those on the moortop by telephone. When I first looked down a shaft, I saw what seemed to be two little pencils, far below; they were the rails.

"I was lowered to the first garland, which I cleared out; then to the second garland, and so on. These garlands fed water into a downspout connected with the main drains of the tunnel. When the man below reported that a train was coming, all I could do was close my mouth and eyes to keep out the smoke. Sometimes, t'smoke took a long time to clear. As it made its way to the tunnel ends or the ventilation shafts, another train would come along and blow it back again..."

Thomas Preston, who worked on the Settle-Carlisle for over fifty years, was fond of recalling when he was sent up to Blea Moor with a message. There had been an explosion below ground. The candle-boy, who took the candles down the shafts, had sustained a broken leg, so Thomas was given the job for a short time. Descending a shaft was one of the most frightening experiences of his boyhood. As he was about to descend, he heard a moorland grouse giving its gutteral call, which sounds like go back, go back. Thomas wished he could take the advice.

The workers in Blea Moor Tunnel needed patience and good lungs. "You used to get smoked up. Iced up, too. First thing of a Monday morning, if it had been freezing and you were the first train through, you'd hear icicles dropping off when you hit 'em...Smoke wasn't so bad unless you'd two or three double-heads through. Then it was a bit choky, but never so bad as some other tunnels I knew.

"If there were plenty o' breeze blowing, it was all right. A permanent way man had recalled going into Blea Moor tunnel and not getting a stroke out of the men because the locomotives were filling the tunnel with smoke and it wouldn't clear. There was a difference of days." In the days of "duck lamps", the old men could tell when a train was entering the tunnel because "it used to suck the flame towards it."

When the track was being lifted with jacks, the existing clearance must not be altered without authority; then there would be a speed restriction. "An old flagman said: 'There's one in.' Ganger chunters. 'I'm telling you, there's one in t'tunnel.' Next thing, ganger looks up, and he's coming. They haven't time to get jacks out. It was just like going over Mount Ararat. The driver stops further down. Ganger runs down and says to him: 'What's thou playin' at? Thou were doing fifty then. Didn't thou see t'slack further back?' He actually got yon driver persuaded he was doing fifty. Driver were so upset, he said to our ganger: 'Don't report me'."

One of the smokiest periods of the tunnel's long life was in the 1939-45 war, when "all this wartime traffic came and filled the place with smoke; you couldn't see your hand before your face. If you got an hour, or an hour and a half's work done in a day, that was quite good. You could get on better on Sunday, when there wasn't much traffic. Through the week, I've seen us do practically nothing.

"You used to get filthy black; you kept old clothes for tunnel work, and chucked 'em away when you'd finished work. You had to stand so close to the wall you'd be touching it, and there was half an inch of soot on the wall. You were black as fireback when you came out. If you left your shovel standing where you were working, then next morning it would be all damp and wet. If you left it for a couple of days, then picked it up, your hands would be filthy.

"At inspection time, a special van was prepared, with scaffolding on top and more scaffolding on part of that in order to let two men inspect the masonry right up against the crown of the tunnel. We invariably set off from Settle, first checked half of Stainforth tunnel and then went to to Blea Moor. About dinner-time we'd have checked half that tunnel, emerging looking like Christie's Minstrels. We'd have a meal, then go on to Dent. Now the line we had been using could be opened up for traffic. The other line was closed, enabling us to complete Blea Moor and Stainforth tunnels on the return to Settle..."

To be in Blea Moor tunnel at track re-laying time was memorable. Naptha lamps were generally used for work in shaft and tunnel, though such a lamp was dangerous, giving off foul fumes. There was a cabin to the south of Blea Moor where naptha was kept. The lamps came in various sizes. There was a rush when work began to get the smaller types, which were of less weight and therefore easier to carry than the standard type.

In mild weather, the workmen could not see for smoke. "Once we got to the middle of the tunnel and we never struck a bat for three days." Smoke went backwards and forwards. Just when we thought it was going to clear, it came back again..."

Said Harry: "Rails go very fast in a tunnel. They used to re-rail Blea Moor every four years. It was the sulphur that caused the damage. In the tunnel, where it was always damp, the loco wheels got to skidding." Rails were taken out and weighed to check on wear. "If they got down to a certain weight, they had to be replaced." In the 1930s, rails were painted before being taken into Blea Moor tunnel. It was an attempt to prolong their working lives."

Forty or fifty of the men had naptha lamps. When a wick had burnt down, a chap would simply knock the lamp against the nearest rail. The force pushed out another inch or two of wick. When Harry worked in Blea Moor, doing shaft work, he and a fellow worker took a pick and excavated, turning up objects like hammer heads and the remains of tools that led him to believe were once held in a blacksmith's shop that stood close to each shaft head.

The workmen built a cabin at the top of each shaft. They could slip into it in bad weather. Such a cabin was entirely home-made from such material as railway sleepers. Men fashioned their own seats. The foreman knocked up a rough cupboard in which he might keep his forms. The tunnel men returned home at week-ends, locking up the cabins. When they realised that some of the many tramps en route across Blea Moor to Dentdale used the cabins at night, they left them unlocked. None of the tramps was known to steal tools.

The workmen on Blea Moor received coal for their fires by way of the shaft. It was wound up from a ballast train below. This way, too, came cement and mortar, which were mixed at the side of the tunnel and raised to the place where it needed. A man dangling in the shaft might shout to his friends if he was near the top or bottom. Otherwise, signals were passed by telephone. There was one in the tunnel and another in the cabin at the top.

Harry said that Rise Hill tunnel, to the north, was "not as bad as Blea Moor". The ganger in Harry's time was George Fawcett, who was also a Wesleyan lay preacher. "He'd be preaching in the chapel on Sunday when he'd spot Jim Atkinson, one of his men. Breaking off from reading the Bible, or preaching, he'd say: "Tunnel in morning, Jim – think on!" Harry recalled when the gang painted the rails. "Three or four men went ahead, washing the rails. We followed, painting them red to preserve them."

Joss Riley was cook for a while. "He knocked off at 11 a.m., an hour before us, and went to the cabin. Outside were our wicker baskets, containing our food. He would take out a thing that had to be warmed, put it on the plate above the fire, and it would be ready for us when we knocked off for dinner at noon. Once he entered the cabin with his naptha lamp. Something went wrong with it. He hurled it outside the cabin. It landed on the wicker baskets. The food went up in flames."

When a hundred trains a day passed through Blea Moor tunnel, conditions were grim. Each locomotive added to the layer of soot and each clogged the air with acrid smoke that found its way

A diverted London to Glasgow Freightliner heads north from Blea Moor tunnel over the summit plateau of the Settle-Carlisle line, which extends for the next ten miles to Ais Gill.

to the ventilation shafts. The shafts were engineering wonders in themselves. As smoke billowed from the circlets of red brick high on the moor it seemed that volcanic times had returned. Blea Moor had become Smoky Mountain.

Northbound, the end of the 1 in 100 "Long Drag" from Settle is immediately inside the tunnel. After climbing 726 feet in fifteen miles – from 425-ft to 1,151-ft – the net height gain over the next ten miles to Ais Gill summit is a mere eighteen feet.

Southbound, an express would thunder down the tracks from Aisgill after its long slog from the Eden Valley. Its whistle startled the hill sheep. It plunged into the blackness of Blea Moor for its 2,629 yards dash some 500-ft below the moor-top. Workmen, hearing the shriek of the train and feeling the compression of air on their eardrums, flattened themselves against the brick lining of the tunnel. Passengers closed the windows of warm compartments and complained of the smell.

The footplate men peered forward, anticipating the circle of light that meant the end of noise and reverberation, of the inky moisture that fell as good clean rain on the roof of Yorkshire. When the train had passed, and the smoke began to find its lazy way to the tunnel mouth and three air shafts, gangers resumed their work of maintaining the track, which was constantly being attacked by moisture and sulphurous fumes.

Fifty years ago, at the northern end of Blea Moor, the author joined a tunnel inspection gang – similar in basic respects to that recalled by Harry Cox. It was early on the grey morning of a wintry day. Mist clung to the hollows. Half the sheep of the district seemed to be on the roads. Railmen who had been working in Blea Moor since a much earlier hour were enjoying hot tea before taking part in the annual tunnel inspection. Standing patiently on the tracks was a cattle wagon with a special framework on top and an ordinary wagon with the customary stock of wedges, cement, sand and brick.

The chief works inspector clambered on to the roof of the cattle wagon with an inspector and three men. They carried small hammers, also spears on long rods. Another inspector settled himself in the other wagon with a sheet of paper on which he would record observations on the state of the tunnel. There was to be no motive power. At a signal from the chief, seven railwaymen put their shoulders to the wagons and sent them rumbling slowly along the track to the tunnel mouth.

I followed closely behind an engineering assistant in the office of the District Engineer at Lancaster. It was relatively cosy in the tunnel. The chilling mist on Blea Moor had been thickening until it had a liquid consistency bordering on drizzle. The tunnel has a crown, haunches and sidewalls. In addition there are tablets on the sidewalls giving the distance from the tunnel mouth at the southern end, so that any part of the masonry might have its position noted exactly.

The men with the hammers tapped continually with the object of locating any 'drummy' [hollow] brickwork. They were keen to know if there was any 'spalling' [soft masonry], which would be knocked down to obviate the risk of it falling on trains. The spearmen probed into joints, their spears being fashioned from worn-out shovels!

The wagons rumbled through the darkness. Paraffin lamps hissed contentedly. From high above the tracks came the chant of the railwaymen as they reported on the state of the brickwork. "Hold it, lads," came a muffled shout. And some soft masonry was brought down, while the position was noted so it might be repaired. The sidewalls were critically examined. They were covered with a mixture of soot, mud and moisture. Said one of the helpers: "Thee wait till we get diesel trains. We're bahn to whitewash the tunnel out when they're rattling about."

From far up the tunnel came three blasts on a whistle. "Train on the down," someone yelled. I felt the compression on my eardrums. There was a shriek from the locomotive. The sound reverberated through the huge cavern. "Clear the six-foot," came another anonymous voice. There was a danger that a wagon sheet was flapping and this might cause severe injuries to anyone in the way if a train was travelling at between fifty and sixty miles an hour.

Another shriek, this time much nearer. A giant locomotive thundered by only a few yards away. Firelight stained the darkness. I heard the staccato clattering of wagons. Then silence – a silence intensified by the smoke that billowed down from the head of the tunnel. The smoke was so thick I could taste it. At this point, at a maxium depth below ground, the first impression created by the passing goods train was of size.

In the open air, trains are invariably dwarfed by the landscape. This huge, moaning monster filled half the tunnel and, it seemed, stretched to within a few inches of the roof. In retrospect, I realised that the smoke in the tunnel was not very thick. Only one train passed through during my visit, the up-line being closed to traffic. And the train I had seen was travelling fast enough to draw most of the smoke behind it.

"Hold it, while it clears a bit, lads," came the anonymous voice. The work was resumed after five minutes. I was told of conditions when there was normal traffic on both lines. "I've known smoke so thick you couldn't see the tilly lamp. Had to feel your way along the tunnel, tapping the line with a piece of stick." How fast the tunnel clears of smoke depends on several factors, including the direction of the wind. A cross-wind might restrict the movement of the smoke. Also the state of the weather. Not forgetting the speed of the trains. A slow train was in the tunnel for a long time. It therefore polluted the atmosphere more than the fast expresses.

I was advised to pull my stockings over the bottoms of my trouser legs. "Otherwise you might find the smoke pouring from under your collar!" I took his advice. The atmosphere was never thick enough that morning to make the precaution necessary. Blea Moor was not a conspicuously dirty tunnel, though the track was replaced every four or five years. The normal life of track in the open is over twenty years.

So we came to Shaft No 3, which at 390-ft from moor to rail level, is 50 feet deeper than the shaft of Gaping Gill, the huge pothole on the flanks of Ingleborough. I was told the shafts are ten feet in diameter and they are marked at intervals by garlands. What seemed to be a spider's web at the head of the shaft was the grill that prevents foreign bodies from falling on to the track.

No 2 shaft proved to be 358-ft deep and No 1 shaft, by far the smallest of the trio, had a depth of 217-ft. The work of re-lining the shaft was taking place; the shaft had been sealed off to prevent

One of the red-brick structures at the head of a shaft, Blea Moor tunnel. Ingleborough lies beyond.

bricks from falling on to the track – and smoke rising to engulf the workmen, who were operating from a cage that dangled at the end of a wire rope attached to a winch on the moor above.

In the depth of winter, water that seeped at the north end of Blea Moor tunnel created impressive icicles, some of which were eighteen inches thick. One aspect of the lengthman's job was to break off the icicles with a long pole. It was a dangerous job. "If you clouted one, you'd shatter it and it'd drop in big lumps." One way of stopping the formation of icicles was to set down some braziers – known as Fire Devils – on the cess side. "A duty man stoked them up. If he wanted more coal, he caught an engine driver's eye and he'd drop some off. Those drivers were glad to see the fires. Driving into big icicles could be dangerous."

In Blea Moor tunnel, someone would point out the frame of a huge gong that was once operated by the trains as they entered the tunnel. Harry Cox spoke about the Donkey Hole – used, it was said, in the construction days. A workman said: "Thou's bin lucky today. Thou'll nobbut need a wesh when thou gets home. Most days I need a bath – aye, an' I've to change t'watter several times an' all."

Outside the tunnel, there would be an ordinary cabin on each length and one near a large viaduct or tunnel. Such cabins were erected by the gangs, each of which contained a fair amount of building talent. Rail sleepers were used for the walls; quite often there was a slate roof. The fireplace extended into the room and had a metal top on which food could be kept warm. Forms were put round the room. There was also a table.

"At one time the foreman would allow a man to go to the cabin an hour before bait [meal] time to prepare food for the men. This man would ask me what I was having. I might reply – half a collop of bacon and a couple of eggs, plus some bread we had got from our lodgings. When bait-time came around, the food would be ready, kept warm on the metal top of the fireplace."

The most memorable Christmas Day Harry Cox spent was 1910. Word came that the Scotch express had been wrecked near Hawes Junction (actually near the viaduct). "We got word on Christmas Eve, shortly after the accident happened and we were soon turning out with the ballast train. We were told to report again at 5 a.m the next day. We would then go up the line to relieve a gang from Carlisle. From a distance we could smell the remains of that express. It was still burning."

Harry remembered Alf Sutton, the signalman whose error led to this major accident. "He was a big Union man, forever exhorting us to join the Union. At one time there were two signal boxes at Hawes, one at each end of the platform. Then the work of these two was brought together in a single box. There was now more than enough work for a signalman." Years later, Harry saw Alf working as a passenger guard on the Morecambe line.

Harry's railway career ended when the powers-that-be decided that apart from lodging away from home in summer this would also be the custom in winter. "It seemed a bit hard," said Harry. "Most of the gang agreed; they were married, and jobs were not easy to come by then. I stuck out and left – friendly enough. My last railway job was to hand in my Rule Book and whistle."

Bill Davison, a former member of the tunnel maintenance gang, who lived for some years at one of the Blea Moor cottages, remembered the Hungry Thirties, when merely having a regular job and somewhere to live was comforting, even if the cottage stood in the wilds, with moorland at the back door. To visit the toilet when home was Blea Moor, one had to go to a small building "at the back". At bath-time, members of the family took turns with a zinc bath that had been laboriously filled with hot water.

Footplate man on a "pick-up". These goods trains stopped at all points along the line and would regularly deliver essential supplies to Blea Moor.

There was no special hardship for Bill's wife, who had been brought up on a farm in Grisedale. In winter she put to good use the skills she had been taught as a girl – knitting, sewing, embroidery, the making of mats and quilts. This family were keen Methodists, members of the society at Horton-in-Ribblesdale, though remoteness meant they could not attend services regularly.

Even so, Bill was a local preacher. When he was planned to preach at Dent, he carried his bike through Blea Moor tunnel – in which he worked on other days of the week – and rode it down the dale to Dent Town, returning by the same route. The Settle-Carlisle had little traffic on Sundays.

Shopping jaunts from Blea Moor took on the flavour of a major expedition. Mrs Davison carried her baby daughter across Ribblehead viaduct to the station beyond, from which it was possible to catch a train to Settle. Groceries were delivered to the station by T D Smiths. They were conveyed to Blea Moor cottages by goods train on one of the regular trips.

The once self-reliant railway community at Blea Moor. The signal box and one cottage remain but the water tank and the two other cottages have now gone.

A Chapel-le-Dale farmer, doing his rounds on horseback, pauses at Blea Moor. The water crane was dismantled many years ago.

Little remains to remind us of the small, self-reliant community of railway folk who lived immediately south of Blea Moor, between the tunnel and viaduct. A signal box presided over some busy "loops" and a number of families coped with life at its simplest, their neighbours being sheep and red grouse. A shepherd did his rounds on horseback. A signalman drove off trespassing sheep which would – he said – be considered by the farmer to be the best in the flock if they were to be struck by a train.

Special gangs were mustered when climatic extremes were expected. The "gale men" gathered south of Blea Moor to await the arrival of a "down" goods train, which was directed into a loop so that the wagon sheets could be checked. Such trains had just crossed the viaduct, where the wind was sometimes strong enough to rip a wagon sheet or even tear a number of sheets away, sending them floating across the fells like autumn leaves – a windfall in a literal sense to any local farmer who was around when they came to earth.

"Snow" men cleared the points and attended to signals obscured by snow. "Cleaning signals was a fair job in itself," said a member of the snow gang. Then there were the "fog men". A man sat in a "lile" cabin near the distant signal. "When t'signal was on, he put a detonator on t'rail. As t'signal came off, he took yon detonator off. If t'distant remained on, and a train went ower it, he cracked it!"

It was not unknown for one man to be a member of more than one gang. A former railwayman remembered a number of times when "it was snowing like hell, and blowing a gale, and you couldn't see the ground!"

The box has a customary feature in a toilet of the Elsan type, set in a compartment "at the top of the steps." A former signalman remarked: "You just went out of the door and turned to t'reet [right]." And there it was, in a handier situation than the old type of toilet – a tin shack a few yards from the box. "It wasn't ower safe in a reet strong wind. I've heard o' one tekkin' off – wi' t'fellow sat there!"

The paraffin lamps were fuelled from a large drum delivered to the lamp house by a friendly neighbourhood freight. "Originally, you'd have a little single-wick lamp above t'book [register]."

Everyone remembered the stove and the kettle, which had a song in its heart from dawn to dusk. "In the old days we had what were called Russell stoves; they had a coal fire and an oven above. We would get a good fire going underneath and put the kettle in the oven."

Blea Moor was continually busy. There were water-cranes. It was a changing over point for loco men. "From about 3 o'clock in the afternoon, sometimes earlier, and reet away through to next morning, you had crews there. Sometimes, if you had a train running late, you'd try to persuade a man to meet the other at Aisgill. Sometimes they'd go and sometimes they wouldn't."

Blea Moor was once "continually busy" with freight trains going into the loops to take water or change crews. This smoky scene shows a Long Meg to Widnes anhydrite train entering the up loop.

Jack Towler, a farm lad who began work on the Settle-Carlisle in the summer of 1924, spent his first day – what turned out to be the first of many days – on Ribblehead viaduct. The ganger, George Cockerill, who had come to this wild part of the north-country from Newmarket, was in charge of a team of five platelayers, men who used muscle-power, not machines, to move rails and sleepers. Most of the gang lived at the row of Victorian cottages erected by the Midland for "railway servants".

Jack adapted himself to an uneasy life on the spectacular viaduct. "You could feel it trembling in certain places when trains were coming over. Frost used to lift the lines up a bit, especially at the southern end." For re-laying work, several gangs were brought together. The work was done by hand. "We'd gangs o' men to pick rails up for loading on to wagons. Then they had to pick 'chaired' sleepers up, six men to a sleeper."

In foggy conditions, a permanent way man might be called out at any time of day or night. During the week that followed the Towlers return from their honeymoon, in 1932, they were living at Salt Lake, fog swirled around the head of the dale and Jack was called out in the middle of the night for fogging duties. He was appointed ganger in 1939, working "by the signal." He was provided with flags, a hand lamp and detonators, which he placed on the line when the signal glowed red.

Salt Lake Cottages, where Jack Towler lived in the 1930s. The six cottages were built by the Midland company for railway servants.

Ribblehead at about the time Jack Towler was working on the line. The massive bulk of Whernside dominates the scene, with the Station Inn nestling in the foreground.

The Ribblehead "foggers" were provided with shelter in the form of huts, two at the north side of the viaduct, for the up and down lines and one towards Selside. Basic facilities were available – a few seats and a stove at which kippers might be toasted. Alf Flack received consignments of "big Scotch kippers" at Ribblehead and sorted them out before going on his rounds of farms and villages. The railwaymen and their families were "partial" to a few kippers. Alf and his family lived at No 6 Salt Lake.

In the 1930s, Salt Lake Cottages, where Jack lived, were owned by the railway company. The property was substantial but basic. No electricity was fitted and after dark the living room held the glow of a paraffin lamp. Bathrooms were what other people had. The Salt Lakers, like so many in those days, bathed in zinc baths before roaring fires. "When you did the washing in the wash-house, you used 'soft' water from the barrel that collected rainwater from the roof," said Mrs Towler.

No water was at hand in the house, apart from the side-boiler in the kitchen range, a boiler that had to be filled by hand. "Many a ton of coal I've shovelled from the road into the coal-house. And many a time I've broken ice on the water-barrel before I could wash." (Electricity and piped water came to the cottages in 1958).

Jack recalled working in Blea Moor tunnel on a Sunday. "Just after I started there, Tommy Preston, who ran the slip and drainage gang, was sent up with the train to unload machinery – winches and that – to go down shafts so that bricklayers could examine them. As platelayers, Jack and his men had to hump the winches over the moor. "There was no easy work in those days."

His main concern was the viaduct. The parapets are so high that a westerly gale passes over the head of the railwayman who is crossing the viaduct. "On a right wet day, you could go on that viaduct and it would be dry." The wildest part was the bank between the station and the viaduct. "It used to blow sheets galore. During t'war they were all tied up wi' bits o' string and all sorts of stuff that wasn't good enough. The wind soon broke 'em."

An engine driver could tell as he arrived at Ribblehead station what the conditions were likely to be at the viaduct. "With a westerly gale, you got gusts coming right down between Ingleborough and Whernside. It was like somebody blowing down a funnel. I used to say to the fireman: 'Look out, I'm going to knock hell out of the engine.' I always kept going, though. Many a time I've looked back and seen wagon sheets being ripped off and just blown away in the wind like pieces of paper...Then you had to stop at Blea Moor. Men were fastening sheets down. Many a time, you got stopped when you wanted to keep going."

The viaduct could be a nightmare in a gale. A fireman said: "The old Class 4 loco hadn't much cab. If the wind was strong, you got your fire prepared before you got on to the viaduct. Then you and your driver got tucked away in a corner and let the engine chuff across." Flying tarpaulins were a hazard peculiar to Ribblehead. "No sheets came off wagons on t'viaduct. They blew down into t'bottom of t'banks. The footplate men had 'em to collect, fold up and put on a bogey to be carted to the station. I've had as many as 100 sheets to pick up. The wind was sometimes strong enough to stop a train. A small loco had to be brought up behind to shove it out."

If a Big Freeze arrived, two platelayers were stationed at each water column day and night to keep the braziers going and thus stop the water in the column from freezing. The men worked a shift system, for weeks on end. "At that time, they had sent some men up from Derby to take all the telegraph poles down between the station and the viaduct – they were going to put the wires in 'boxing' – and those men were up there for six weeks and never did a 'bat'. They couldn't get in for frost."

The wintry spell of early 1947 is well remembered for days that were calm and clear, with a blue sky. The wind that blew at night undid any efforts of the previous day's snow-cutting. Salt Lake was cut off for eight weeks by road. "We had the railway telephone and they would ring up if there was a train due. This gave us time to get to the platform. Traffic went no further than the special 'snow platform'."

Snow has always been a factor in life at Ribblehead and Blea Moor. This view of snow-clearing operations at Ribblehead station dates from Midland Railway days.

Glasgow to London express snowbound between Risehill and Blea Moor tunnels in 1963.

Snow-clearers north of Blea Moor tunnel.

Locomotive buried in a drift with only the chimney visible!

The cutting between the viaduct and Blea Moor was soon filled with snow. A special snow-clearing train came up. "One of these fire-blowers. It came on Saturday morning. As per usual, when it got there and they got it fixed up, it wouldn't go. When it eventually set off, they made arrangements for all t'points to be 'clipped' at Blea Moor. It was going straight through to Dent. It got to t'cutting at Blea Moor and when it touched snow it didn't go more than a few yards. It blew a bit o'snow out of the base. And it blew ballast all over t'moor. What they thought was snow was really all ice!"

A locomotive inspector who rode with the crew when they were snow-ploughing was new to the line; he turned up wearing a blue Melton overcoat, smart suit, a homberg and rubber boots. Usually, an inspector in those conditions had donned his oldest clothes, slipped an old donkey jacket over them and had reached for a pair of wellingtons.

In 1947, prisoners of war were brought up in ballast trains to clear snow out of Ribblehead station. The snow was emptied over the parapets of the viaduct. "I remember one lot of prisoners arriving; they wouldn't get out of the train to clear snow. When eventually the inspector got them out and got the wagons filled and took them to t'viaduct, they wouldn't empty t'wagons. The inspector was a very religious man; and they 'turned' him. I never heard a man swear as much in all my life! He said: 'If my wife could hear me now, she'd drop down dead!'"

Jack worked twelve hours a day, and when he came home at night he went straight into the kitchen, took his coat off and it stood up by itself! He was off work with frost-bitten nose and ears after that.

Trains were brought to a halt at the bridge near Salt Lake Cottages. "Of course, we used to walk up and have a look at them," said Mrs Towler. "One of the drivers shouted: 'Do you want some black snow?' I didn't realise what he meant but I said: 'Oh, yes please.' He brought me half a sack of coal. We had a pig killed. So I exchanged bacon for coal."

In wartime, two sidings at Blea Moor were replaced by loops, theoretically to ease the traffic flow at a time when it was heavy. "Those loops caused a lot of bother." There were runaways – wagons containing iron ore, sugar, beer, once even explosives. Fortunately, the trucks remained on the rails and came to a halt between Settle and Long Preston. Also during the war, the Home Guard mounted guard over Ribblehead viaduct, which would be a prime target for enemy aircraft.

Robert and Denis Taylor, members of the Home Guard, were regularly on duty at the viaduct. The base was a hen-hut next to the massive structure. The weapons of those on duty were a wooden gun and the shaft of a pickaxe. Denis was the despatch rider who also spent one night a week in a wooden hut on Burnmoor. Mobility was provided by a BSA single-cylinder 250 motorbike. A Clapham member of the Home Guard who became familiar with Ribblehead ended his spell of duty in the waiting room at the station. Asked if he had left a bullet in the rifle, he shook his head, pointed the rifle upwards, pulled the trigger – and sent a bullet careering through the ceiling and slates into the starlit sky yonder.

When Queen Elizabeth (subsequently the Queen Mother) travelled on the Settle-Carlisle in the royal train, it was to rest overnight at Dent station. In advance of its arrival, the local policeman stood on the bridge near Salt Lake and men were on duty at every Blea Moor shaft. Jack Towler was stationed at Ribblehead. "Some cows came off t'pick-up [train] at night and were put into pens, ready for t'farmers next morning. Just before the royal train was due on its way to Dent, these cows – having broken out – were found wandering on the line and down towards Salt Lake. We had to run after 'em and get 'em back...We got 'em back just before she landed."

During the war, "there were derailments, one after another – maybe two a week." Two ammunition wagons came off at Ribblehead box. "They'd jumped t'line. We'd to get troops to come to move them." Enemy aircraft droned overhead as they quested for Ribblehead or Denthead viaducts. Alf Flack reported having gone out at night into a field to watch flares descending near the viaduct. Bombs were heard.

Mrs Towler relates: "We went to bed about 10 o'clock one night – it was the time the planes went to Belfast – and the sound was terrible all night through...We sat in the house one night. My niece and her husband were living with us; they had just got a baby. We let them have the front room. I heard a plane approaching and said: 'Out with those lights in there.' It wasn't three minutes before the plane was back again; it had dropped bombs at Cloughton brickworks. We heard the bang."

Jack and his men were returning from working at Blea Moor at 5 p.m on a misty day. "We got as far as Ribblehead and heard a big aeroplane coming over, droning away. I says: 'He'll have to look out, the way he's going.' We didn't get much further when there was such a bang. A Lancaster bomber had crashed into Whernside."

Next morning, Jack looked through the staircase window on to the fell and saw the remains of the huge plane. The five crew members perished; their bodies were reverently carried to Winterscale Farm and placed in the sitting room until they were claimed by the RAF. Jack added: "You wouldn't think there'd be as much life at a little place like Ribblehead."

George Horner, former signalman at Blea Moor, with his model of the "Contractor's Hotel".

The finished model displayed alongside Ribblehead viaduct.

In 1953, George Horner made the acquaintance of the remote and gale-blasted Blea Moor signal box. "When I'd been at Ribblehead for six to eight months, there was a temporary summer relief job and one of t'lads out of Blea Moor box went out on that. So I went to Blea Moor for t'summer. I remember the date because that summer the express piled up there. It happened in the afternoon when I was t'night man."

Those who manned the Blea Moor signal box were among the unsung heroes. They trudged beside the tracks for a mile or so from viaduct to signal box. They rarely lacked company. The ganger and his merry men sometimes handed over tins of food with the request that they might be warmed up on the signal box stove by noon. (One man laughed when the tins were collected. It was the first time he had eaten boiled pears.)

Untypically, one signalman at Blea Moor box regarded his task with levity and humour. He referred to the tunnel, even to Control, as the "Toob". He applied for a vacancy at Garsdale but failed on the telegraph instrument. He remarked that if an instrument could be found with a rubber needle – presumably to erase his errors – he was sure he could pass. He swatted his hairless chest with his towel when washing – to draw attention to his likeness to a robin redbreast!

The noted photographer and 'Railway Bishop', Eric Treacy, had a special affection for Blea Moor. He took this image from the footplate of a locomotive leaving Ribblehead and heading for Blea Moor tunnel.

Among those calling at Blea Moor box were engine crews, waiting to change trains, or members of the special duty gangs. Railway enthusiasts, including the 'Railway Bishop', Eric Treacy, had a special love for the Blea Moor box. From time to time, walkers lost on the fells at the coming of night were attracted to the box by the lamplight.

The box was not of the familiar Midland type. Early in the 1939-45 war, the layout of the tracks was changed from back-in sidings to loops. The original signal box, set beside the "down" line, was replaced by a box of late LMS period, in which the levers are close together. There is a left-hand frame, so the signalman, when working the levers, must face the back wall instead of looking directly through the front window.

The original Midland signal box at Blea Moor stood beside the down line.

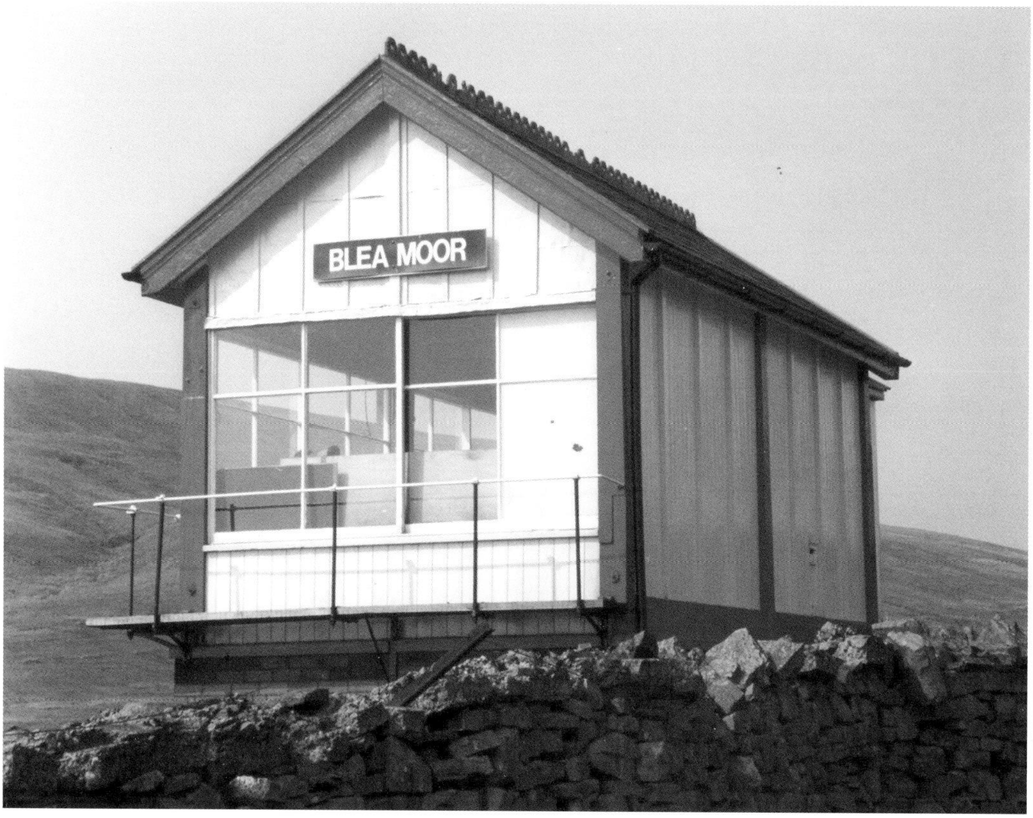

Blea Moor signal box as it is today.

Neville Caygill in Blea Moor box. He had a twenty-minute walk from where he left his car.

George recalled: "If a signal lamp failed, the signalman at Blea Moor sent for the lamp-man, if one was available. Otherwise, it was the signalman's duty to attend to a lamp. He'd find a 'slack' time, tell his mates on either side that he was going to change a lamp – and off he went to change it."

George, attending to a "dead" lamp, might be up the distant signal, which stood at the end of the viaduct, at midnight. "It was t'best time to do it. You couldn't see t'floor. You didn't know how high you were. In daylight, you'd notice there was about a hundred foot down. It wasn't a very tall signal, this down distant, but it stood on top of t'bank. In a strong gale, that signal fairly waggled when you got to the top."

The job at Blea Moor box was temporary. It would end when two lads returned from doing their National Service. When, indeed, the job did end, two years later, George returned to "the traffic side." His Dad had secured a job as signalman at Blea Moor. George, junior, eventually joined the elite group of men who had held this position. He and his father were working together.

Their transport from Salt Lake was the push-bike. "If it was ower-wild for a bike, we walked. It can be hellish on by Gunnerfleet when the wind begins to funnel under t'viaduct." Father took his bike up to the box. "The ballast was kept tidy then; he was able to cycle and then carry his bike across the tracks to the box." George was inclined to leave his bike near the viaduct.

Said George: "I suppose all thirty levers in the box were used at one time. Maybe most of them still are." George and Blea Moor box became attached on a permanent basis in the late 1950s. "We were there at t'transition period when they were changing from steam to diesel...At that time you didn't always go by class. You'd ask t'bloke behind what's this divvil got on? Is he a steamer or a diesel? You had to go against convention and decide which was fastest and which should have the 'road'. At latter end, it got a bit of a mess wi' t'steam. They didn't do all that weal and diesels were new.

"Of course, we had trouble wi' diesels.The thing about an old steamer was that it might not do ower well now and again, especially when there was bad coal, or summat like that, but it always managed to twine itself to t'next signalbox, so that they could get at 'im. In early days, if a diesel decided to lay doon, it lays doon where it is! And you've lost 'im."

For the night shift, George had to be at Blea Moor at 10 p.m. "Unless it was a brilliant moonlit night – which, of course, you did get from time to time – you needed a torch. If you were on 2 till 10, you'd see your mate coming to relieve you. You'd see his leet coming over t'hill."

The signal box shared a water supply with the houses. "It had a tap at t'bottom of t'steps. This was a great thing. The water came off Whernside. There was a tank set up and it had a pipe going in and a pipe coming out. A 'rose' over t'end stopped foreign bodies going through. It did get bunged up from time to time.

The changeover from steam to diesel had its moments – even at Blea Moor. This manic scene dates from 11 August 1968, when what was officially billed as "the last steam train on British Railways" paused to the accompaniment of clicking cameras.

Diesels were soon to the fore and gained their own devotees. This class 40 is heading an enthusiasts' special at Blea Moor.

Originally, there would be a single-wick lamp over the record book. "They always used to say that if there was too much leet in t'box you couldn't see what was going on outside. Not that you could see a lot if it was dark, anyway ... Main thing you looked for after dark was a hot axle-box...After a bit, we got hanging Aladdin lamps. Then we got quite modern. They gave us Tilly lamps."

A signalman on the Drag, the first fifteen miles of the Settle-Carlisle, became an authority on hot axle-boxes. A wheel was solid on its axle. The whole lot turned. An axle box was in two halves, fastened up with bolts. If you got a divided box, where a bolt came loose and the bottom half dropped away, that was the half that had the oily pad. It then overheated. It could get so hot as to strike fire. You would see it visibly blazing.

"When a box burnt out, the next thing you got was a 'squealer'," George explained. "You would hear it. Now and again, if you went to t'door as a train was going by, you could even smell it. A neglected hot axle box led to an end being cut off and the vehicle dropping on to the wheel." Then, George added, it was off the road!

He recalled the old-style Russell stove, which had a coal fire in t'bottom and an oven on top. Said George: "The idea was to get a good fire going and put kettle in t'oven. You'd get it boiling and then pull it to t'front to get it off t'main o' t'heat. It used to sing away all day. You kept topping him up. You could always get a brew at a signal box. Particularly at Blea Moor." A new system was developed when "they" took out the old stove and installed an ovenless Courtier stove. No electricity was provided. Lighting was courtesy of a paraffin lamp.

Sheep, looking for a toothsome bite of grass on the banks, strayed on to railway property. "There were not as many killed as you might think when you noticed how many sheep got onto t'track from time to time. A lot of sheep were lambed on t'railway side. They were brought up there. It was home! The engineers might get the sheep off and go back to Ribblehead. By the time they were half-way back, the blooming sheep had returned..."

George's favourite sheep story was of an old sheep that was laid in the four-foot [the space between the tracks]. "There were no trains about, and none expected for half an hour. There was no point in going down and chessin' the sheep off. This old lady lying in the four-foot was quite content chewing her cud.

"An inspector entered the box. He said: 'What about that sheep there – don't you think you should get it off?' I said: 'Let her stop theer.' He said: 'She'll get run over.' I said: 'It's her bloody look-out.' I were a bit more accustomed to sheep than he was. She was lying, chewing her cud, when t'night express was offered. I got it on t'line and I pulled off.

"The inspector, who was keeping his eye on the sheep, said: 'Now then, it's not right, isn't this. Go and get her off!' 'Blow her,' I said, 'she's right where she's at.'"

George had visions of what would happen. He had seen it before. The story continued: "In a bit there was a rumbling and this big yellow nose on t'express came under t'bridge. Sheep was still there. The inspector said: 'I can't watch this.' But he couldn't resist.

"As the express came, he turned again to look at the sheep. She got up, stretched and walked out of the way. Express shot by her at about sixty miles an hour. Then she went and got back into t'road and lay down again. The inspector said that if anyone had told him that would happen, I'd have called him a liar."

George recalled when the Dawson family lived in one of the railway cottages at the trackside. On the other side of the house was the boundless moor. Said George: "Old Jack Dawson, who lived up at Blea Moor, and was ganger up in t'tunnel, knew all about the water system. You'd just mention to Jack that t'watter was petering out and he'd say in his slow, calm voice: 'I'll go and see to it.' And he did. That was the last you heard of Jack. Next thing you knew, t'watter had landed."

Jack Dawson, ganger at Blea Moor.

Jack, whose real name was John, was a member of the Tunnel Gang at Blea Moor who did not see daylight during the working day in winter. "He used to go into the tunnel in the early morning, when it was dark, and he'd come out in the late afternoon, when it was dark. On so many weeks in the year, he was always in the dark. He got 9s a week extra on his wage. This was known to the men as "muck money".

Nancy Edmondson (née Dawson) recalled with pride and some amusement incidents from her upbringing. At Christmastide, 1939, the Dawson family – John Stainton Dawson, his wife and three daughters Edith, Margaret and Nancy -- moved from Salt Lake Cottages, just south of Ribblehead station, to No 1 of two cottages that stood twixt the rail tracks and moorland.

Nancy relates that Dad, the aforementioned Jack, retired from railway service in about 1956. A few sticks of rhubarb in the plot that was a garden are a reminder of the days when he was a keen gardener in an unpromising setting. Workwise, as a ganger, he and his mates operated on the length that began half way across Ribblehead viaduct and took in half of Blea Moor tunnel. He knew the highs and lows of his occupation. On the viaduct he was at an elevation of rather more than 100-ft. In the tunnel he was around 500-ft below the crest of the moor. His job was regularly to check the line and effect any minor repairs.

At the house allocated to the Dawson family, there were two downstairs rooms – a living room and a front room which was used only rarely, when visitors came – and three upstairs rooms containing beds. A coal fire in the kitchen was sustained by an allowance of coal brought by rail and dumped at the trackside, from where it was transported to the wash-house.

Mum went to Settle by rail on Tuesdays, which were market days. Groceries were delivered from Dent village. With no running water in the house (but with a cold water supply in the washhouse across the yard) life was spartan. In the kitchen was one of the big black ranges, with a fireplace incorporating a hot-water boiler.

This was particularly handy for washing or when, on bath night, a tin bath was set before the fire and a copious supply of heated water was required. Father had an aversion to bathing. Not until he retired and the family moved to Winshaw was a bathroom available. He bathed once, then said: "If that's bathing, I don't think I'll bother any more." He was as good as his word.

In due course, Nancy, who was eighteen months old when the move took place to Blea Moor, attended the primary school in Chapel-le-Dale. At the age of five, she and others followed a one and a-half mile long moorland track to the road at Ribblehead. A bus conveyed them to school.

"My sister Margaret told me that, on windy days, when I was liable to be blown over while walking under one of the viaduct arches, I was to fill the hem of my coat with stones. It was so much easier to walk on the railway line; we knew the times of the trains and could identify the signals. There were little recesses we could step into if, very occasionally, a train was imminent."

Nancy Dawson at Blea Moor. She and her sisters spent much time on trains that stopped specially for them. Her elder sister left for her wedding on the footplate of a locomotive!

When Nancy, at 11-plus, began to attend Settle Girls' High School, there were anxious times in winter, when the dale road was clogged with snow. One morning, the bus was driven as far as Salt Lake Cottages. Further progress was hampered by snowdrifts. "With snow heaped on either side of the road, the bus driver had to reverse all the way from Salt Lake almost to Ribblehead."

The Blea Moor children spent much time in the signalbox, which – in their isolation - was the only place to which they might go. "We children spent a lot of time with the signalmen. We were not supposed to 'work' the box – but we did! Such as when the signalman went outdoors to clean the windows. A signalman, in a quiet time, went for a swim in the water-tower. I kept an eye on things while he was away from the box." Harold Thoresby doubled as the local barber. Anyone who wanted a haircut visited the signal box for a "short back and sides". He was equally good attending to the hair of women.

The Blea Moor folk lived at a time of grim winters. They were cold and snowy. Nancy could not recall a bad summer. Most of the summer holidays were spent haymaking at nearby farms. They were familiar with the walk from Blea Moor to Ribblehead station. If they wore wellingtons and a wind was blowing, the tops of their legs were red-raw.

Father visited the Station Inn on Friday evenings. He drank a few pints and played a few games of dominoes. Nancy recalls: "My mother always worried about him coming back because he walked on the railway, in the dark. He was very late one night so she went out to look for him." On the last stretch of his homeward walk, he had left the railway and used the lineside footpath, which runs behind the signal box to the back of the house. He entered the house, locked the door and went upstairs to bed while his wife was still looking for him. Returning to a locked door, she had to knock to gain admission. Father, opening the door, said: "What's ta doing out theer?"

Nancy's eldest sister, Edith, was married while the Dawsons were at Blea Moor. The wedding ceremony took place at Chapel-le-Dale church. "You couldn't get ready for a wedding at Blea Moor. We all went down to Ribblehead. My sister got her hair put in curlers and was then lifted on to a railway engine, disembarking at Ribblehead and getting ready for the ceremony at the Station Inn."

Margaret, the middle sister, and her family, lived in a newer house at Blea Moor. When she was expecting her third baby, and went into labour, the only course of action was to stop an express train and get a lift to Settle station. She was helped on to the chosen train with difficulty. Dad got below her, the train guard held her from above – and they heaved her aboard. At Settle, she was transferred to Cawder Gill hospital at Skipton, where her son Christopher was born.

The Dawsons of Blea Moor occasionally visited a daughter at Newcastle-on-Tyne. They travelled by rail, of course, and on the return journey, waiting for a connection at Carlisle station, they would usually see a train crew known to them. The railmen, who knew John Dawson and his lassies, would say: "We'll stop at Ribblehead and let you off." They were as good as their word and the family dismounted under the surprised gaze of other passengers. Nancy recalls lots of trips on the trains. "They were often stopping at Blea Moor for water or some other reason."

Hens and pigs provided the family with some basic foods. "We were never short of bacon and eggs." When a pig was to be slaughtered, a farmer from Winterscales Farm was summoned to do the work. It was wartime. Rationing was in force. Pig-meat was hidden in a bath-trub which stood in the porch at the front door. This entry, being on the moorland side, was rarely used. Father was a good gardener; there was a steady supply of potatoes and vegetables.

The water supply originated at the beck which flowed over an aqueduct, above the railway. It was sparkling, hard water off the limestone. "There were a few tiny animals in it here and there. If you got a dead sheep in the stream, someone had to go and clean it out. The household toilet was at the end of the washhouse, across the yard; it was an earth-type – just a great hole in the ground with a seat on top...Someone came, now and again, and dug it out." At night-time, when it was dark, we went in two's and three's."

Eventually, the railway authorities decided the family should have chemical toilets. "Dad took a long time looking at this thing when it was installed. He weighed-up what it entailed, then said: 'Those who use it can empty it.' He disappeared from sight up the fell, visiting a pothole. Going to the toilet at night was a trial. The short journey was made by candlelight, a ladin-can [metal container] being placed over part of the candle on a windy night so the flame would not be blown out. Tilly lamps, fuelled by paraffin, were used in the main rooms of the house.

During the wintry spell early in 1947, the Dawsons were in a white desert and Nancy was not able to attend school for twelve weeks. Visually, it was a spectacular winter. It snowed at night and froze all day, so the snow got deeper and firmer. "You were just walking on the top of the latest snowfall. Every morning we had to dig out from the back door so that we could go outdoors and get water. We had a good supply of food. Groceries were delivered."

In his railway work, John Dawson battled to keep the points open. "That winter, when he came into the house during the night, his eyebrows were like icicles and his greatcoat was iced up. Conditions became so bad, the cutting leading to the tunnel was blocked and the railway line was closed. Then we heard about a fantastic snow-clearing machine that was going to come through. [It was a revolutionary jet engine on a flat truck]. On its appearance, 'twas said, snow would fly in all directions. It would be dangerous to be out and about. Everyone must stay indoors."

Nancy and her mother went upstairs so they might see this marvellous snow-clearer from a bedroom window. Dad, unimpressed, said: "There's nothing'll shift it except a lot o' men wi' shovels." He sat at the siding, smoking his pipe, sure that "It'll never come up here." It never appeared. Italian prisoners were brought in to clear the cutting of snow.

It was hard work going to Winterscales farm for a can of milk. There were 4-ft snowdrifts. "Wherever there was thick vegetation, such as rushes, under the snow, your legs sank. It took ages to walk that quarter of a mile." At other times of the year, it was pleasant to follow the path over Blea Moor to a small cottage at Cowgill near the viaduct where Granny, who lived in Leeds, stayed during holiday times. During the walk over the Moor, they passed the circular, red-brick structures at the head of the shafts that ventilated the tunnel.

"Dad was supposedly on guard there whenever a royal train was due. It was in case no one threw anything down the shaft as the train passed. Dad went out, pottered about, then came back. There didn't seem much point in going far. You rarely saw anyone." An exception was a tramp they nicknamed Two Spoonfuls. He called on the Dawsons now and again. Dales hospitality ensured he was offered a cup of tea. He always asked for two spoonfuls of sugar to sweeten it.

Ribblehead station in the glory days of steam. When Nancy Dawson was at Blea Moor the waiting room was the venue for dances and monthly Sunday services.

When Nancy referred to a social life, of sorts, at Ribblehead station, she had in mind the times when the waiting room was the venue for dances, music being provided by George Horner, with top musical talent – on gramophone records. Worship was a part of local life during the construction of the line. Under the impulse of the Victorian "moral conscience", the Midland and Mr Ashwell, the contractor, set up nonsectarian mission stations. The chosen missionary was esssentially "one with a loving heart and a desire to do the people good." Clergymen, if they wished, "could appear in canonicals and might read church prayers before the sermon."

In the spiritual update, recalled by Nancy, her family and friends, the Vicar of Ingleton officiated at the monthly Sunday services which took place in a waiting room heated by coal fire and illuminated by oil lamp. Music was provided by harmonium, the instrument usually standing in a corner of the room. The vicar stood with his back to the ticket window and used the ticket barrier as his pulpit. For the lesson, the Bible was set on a music stand. Conveniently, the station was closed for business on that day, though prayers might be disturbed by the clatter of a through train or the howling of the wind at this venue over 1,000-ft above sea level. The peak congregation was at the Harvest Festival.

Nancy recalls that when Dad retired, it was time for everyone to move from Blea Moor. It was a sad experience, for there had been Dawsons at the house by the tracks for seventeen years. Nancy left Settle Girls High School and took up work in a hospital at Newcastle-on-Tyne. She says, reflectively: "We enjoyed Blea Moor and look back on it with fondness..."

The most dramatic moment in Nancy's life at Blea Moor was when, aged 14, she was sun-bathing on the roof of the pig-sty – when the Thames-Clyde express was derailed – a few hundred yards away from where she sat. It was Eastertime, 21 April, in 1952. Nancy heard a scraping sound and the noise of gushing steam. "When I sat up, all I could see was steam. Then I saw a locomotive on its side and the first three coaches lying at strange angles."

The up express, a ten-coach train, had left Glasgow at 9-15 a.m. The engine was a class 7P 4-6-0 Number 46117 Welsh Guardsman, piloted by a class 4 ex-Midland Compound No 41040. As events turned out, it was fortunate that the coaches had steel underframes. The climb to Aisgill went well. A permanent slack of 15 mph obtained beyond but as the train entered Blea Moor tunnel its speed had increased to 45 mph. Members of the permanent way gang in the tunnel noticed that "something" on the leading engine was striking the ballast. They were, however, powerless to call attention to this. On the engine, nothing amiss had been noted by either the footplate crew or an instructor who was travelling with them.

At 1.23 pm, a brake rod on the compound loosened at one end, causing it to rotate, striking the ballast. If the train had been on plain track, only superficial damage would have ensued. Alas, at the facing points leading into the up loop at Blea Moor, the rod struck the lock stretcher bar, causing the blades to move beneath the train engine. The results were disastrous.

The pilot engine remained on the track and though its tender was derailed it remained upright. Welsh Guardsman fell on its near side. This led to the first four coaches being thrown off their bogies, blocking all lines. The following four coaches, though derailed, remained upright. And the last two remained on the track.

Nancy made for the scene of the accident. She found a carry-cot containing a baby who happily was unharmed. The mother scrambled out of one of the side windows of a carriage and was re-united with her child. "People started coming out of the coaches. No one seemed to be badly hurt, though there were injuries caused by flying glass." She then found a boy who had been thrown through a window; his legs were lacerated below the knees. Other people were sitting around.

In fact, the train had almost 200 passengers. Injuries in the main were light, though seventeen passengers needed hospital treatment. The modern stock of the train ensured that in these circumstances there were no fatalities. The first reaction of Nancy's mother to news of the accident had been to "put the kettle on for cups of tea". She then tore sheets and pillowcases into strips to bandage up those who were bleeding.

Such was the situation of the crashed train; it was some time before a rescue party arrived. The ambulance men had a shock on reaching the scene, for – as noted – it was a hot day at Easter. Passengers who were not injured were lying flat, sunbathing, their inert forms giving an impression to the new arrivals that they were dead. Nancy received a letter of congratulation from the Girl Guides' Association and a watch from the railway authority.

Incidentally, on the day of the accident, three cranes were at the site by 5-30 pm., single line working was introduced at 9-12 am next day and by 4-40 pm, normal service on the Settle-Carlisle line was resumed.

MINISTRY OF TRANSPORT

RAILWAY ACCIDENTS

REPORT ON THE DERAILMENT
which occurred on
18th April 1952 at
BLEA MOOR
Between Dent and Ribblehead in the
LONDON MIDLAND REGION
BRITISH RAILWAYS

LONDON : HER MAJESTY'S STATIONERY OFFICE
1952

SIXPENCE NET

Chapter Seven

Saving the Railway - Portakabins and Portaloo at Ribblehead – The Viaduct is re-born – A mass walk.

In the 1980s, a temporary settlement appeared at Ribblehead. It consisted of several smart, shiny, metal buildings of the collect and re-locate variety – Portakabins and a Portaloo: here today and gone to another job in the foreseeable future. The Victorian hutments were spread over a wide area. This latest group stood close to the piers, separated from open ground by barriers of bright plastic material.

On site was the office and workplace of Tony Freschini, the Project Resident Engineer. Attached to an office wall were photocopies of the original Midland plans for what became known as Ribblehead viaduct. Tony must check them carefully. Victorian engineers did not always work precisely according to plan. On a table in the office were cores taken from the viaduct – cores of limestone from the piers and either red or blue brick from under the arches. The last named, made from local clay at the time of construction, were pitted with small holes and held particles of "foreign material".

Tony Freschini. the railway engineer who supervised the extensive restoration of Ribblehead viaduct.

During a 34-year-long railway career, Tony had held a variety of posts with British Rail's civil engineering department. For six months he organised the repair of fire damage at Summit Tunnel, Todmorden, at a total cost of £1,250,000. On the Settle-Carlisle, he used modern techniques to build Bridge 245, spanning the new Appleby by-pass. He was now applying his energy and skills to the celebrated Bridge 66 – Ribblehead viaduct.

Elsewhere on the site were living and toilet facilities – all of the mobile type – though the majority of the workforce were commuters, their homes situated within fifty miles of Ribblehead. The scaffolders, who had overlaid the viaduct with a web-like structure of rods and planks, were resident, having their own little enclave. This was approached under an arch formed of scaffolding. A water tank rested on a scaffolded tower.

A Wigan man who was in charge of the team allowed me to see inside their quarters, which were luxurious compared with the standards of the 1870s, when the viaduct was under construction. Steps of scaffolding led to the door of their residence, which consisted of rest room, kitchen and bedroom with four orthodox bunk beds and – to accommodate any extra men foisted on them – a two-decker bunk fashioned, as you would expect, from scaffolding and planks. Television was available and, this being a male resort, a few saucy pictures adorned the walls.

Behind the newly erected scaffolding, the viaduct looked firm but careworn. Metal plates had been installed following repairs to piers and spandrel area. Piers 7 and 9 had unsightly re-strapping and girdling, its old-time splendour lost with this engineering corsetry. The name Midland was now just an item for the history books. For a time, that company, with its smart new all-weather railway extending from Settle to Carlisle, and a slogan "Midland for Comfort", had provided more daytime trains than did its rival on the Lancaster-Carlisle route, via Shap.

In an editorial, The Times made a special point of stressing comfort. The opening of the Settle-Carlisle would not only improve access to Scotland to those living in the south-west; it would enable travellers from the south to go north with unaccustomed comfort, even luxury. The Westmorland Gazette extolled the landscape beauty, observing that "the Pullman cars and the new rolling stock offer great advantages, their windows allowing a wider range of outlook than can be obtained from a common carriage."

When, in 1923, there was grouping under the LMS title, the Midland and the London & North Western were absorbed and it was the London to Glasgow route via Shap, rather than the Settle-Carlisle, that became pre-eminent.

A shiver went through the railway world in 1948 with nationalisation. To the men at the top, the Settle-Carlisle was now just a duplicate line. With the through route to Glasgow shared by several regions, the old Midland route went into steady decline. In the 1950s, small stations on the Settle-Carlisle were closed.

Not so Ribblehead station, which since the 1930s had been a prime weather-reporting point, one of the few in highland England. On each hour during the day, a coded message was sent to an R A F air station in Yorkshire for transmission to the Air Ministry's weather station at Dunstable. With a complete picture of Britain's weather before them, the meteorologists were able to make a confident prediction of the weather for the whole country.

In December, 1953, when the Settle-Carlisle was still accommodating a hundred trains a day, most of them freight, the author visited Mr M A Elliot, the stationmaster who was also a weather-recorder. It was a day on which the rain lashed down in true Pennine form. A wind velocity of eight knots was indicated on instruments in the station office. Mr Elliot said a wind speed of 50 knots was common. There had been days when the dial showed 70 knots and blustering winds had blown to a halt trains crossing the viaduct, especially freight trains.

Cattle wagons were notoriously difficult to operate when battered by the wind. An improbable, oft-repeated story concerned a man who, walking on the viaduct, lost his cap to a frolicsome wind. The cap was blown under one of the arches and up the other side. It plopped back on his head – the wrong way round!

At a much later date, a railway guard, referring to Ribblehead's notoriety for keen winds, said he had seen cars blown over the side. "We had several wagons loaded with them one wild night. Halfway over the viaduct, there was a sudden terrific shower of sparks. When we got to Dent box, the signalman shouted: 'Lads! Three of them Humber Snipes is missing!' And by heck they were. We found them at first light – just scrap metal down in the stream bed."

Ribblehead as a weather station with coded details being telephoned to the Air Ministry.

Bill Sharpe, stationmaster-cum-meteorologist.

Mr Clark, stationmaster at Ribblehead, releasing a hydrogen balloon to determine the height of the cloud layers.

When the author called at Ribblehead station in 1953, there was no rain gauge, though one was to be installed ere long. Estimating the height of clouds was relatively easy. The elevation of Ingleborough and Whernside were known precisely. When there was some doubt about the cloud height, a hydrogen-filled balloon was released from the station platform. The rate of climb was known. It was now just a matter of observing how long it took to reach the cloud – and applying some simple mathematics.

Wartime – and the viaduct was a prime target for German aircraft out to cripple the economy by selective bombing. Trainloads of United States troops, complete with jeeps, were seen travelling south, having disembarked from ships by the Clyde. American soldiers lobbed packets of gum to any station staff they saw. In grim weather, a Lancaster bomber just missed the viaduct and plunged into the flank of Whernside with a loss of the air crew, whose bodies were temporarily moved to a nearby farmhouse, awaiting collection.

The LDV (officially the Local Defence Volunteers, unofficially Look, Duck and Vanish) patrolled the viaduct, a prime target for enemy aircraft. Two members of the Taylor family – Robert and his brother Dennis – were among members of the voluntary force, which became officially known as the Home Guard. As they went on patrol, they had one of the few available rifles.

As mentioned, a Clapham man reported back to the station, stood in the waiting room and was asked if the barrell of the rifle was clear of ammunition. Of course it was! He demonstrated by pulling the trigger. Instead of a simple click there was a deafening report – and a bullet zoomed through the roof, shattering one or two slates in its skyward progress.

Two 1960 views of Ribblehead viaduct, when the structure was starting to show signs of wear and tear. Three years later the Beeching Report recommended the withdrawal of passenger services over the line.

The Beeching Report, issued in 1963, took a savage approach to the re-structuring of British Rail and recommended the withdrawal of all passenger services from the Settle-Carlisle. Happily, these proposals were shelved, though by May 1970, the system looked shabby, the passenger service was a meagre two-trains-a-day in each direction and the only stations left open were at Settle and Appleby West. There was still a modicum of freight, even less through the 1970s, when little money was invested and most freight traffic was switched to the West Coast route.

The run-down continued through the 1970s, as instanced by the neglected state of Ribblehead station.

British Rail, disinclined to meet the cost of renewing major features like Ribblehead Viaduct and Blea Moor tunnel, began to use the alleged poor state of Ribblehead as an excuse for closing the line. Yet the centenary of the line was joyfully celebrated in 1976. There was a quibble from H Weston, of Bingley, who wrote to The Dalesman about a misconception, originating in the 1880s, about the height of Ribblehead viaduct.

Mr Weston observed that in Williams's book The Midland Railway: Its Rise and Progress the height was stated to be 165-ft from the bottom of the foundations to rail level. This had been accepted as fact but, wrote Mr W, is "demonstrably not true...It is only necessary to drop a surveyor's tape from the parapet of the highest pillar to show that the rails are 100-ft above ground."

Clement E Stretton, in The History of the Midland Railway, had got it right in 1901. "The implication is that rail level is 140-ft above the ground. This is not correct at the present time and it is inconceivable that the ground level has altered 40-ft in the intervening years. It is undoubtedly a fact that the present height of the rails above ground level is approximately 100-ft."

E H Thompson, of Mirfield, spoke up for Blea Moor Tunnel, which – he noted - would surely rank as one of the big jobs in this great feat of railway construction. A glance at the map would show that most of the famous railway tunnels in Yorkshire lie within easy reach of a road that would assist the contractor in his problems. "Blea Moor could offer only the Ingleton-Hawes road, which was a good distance from the scene of action."

In 1981, opposition to the closure became channelled into a lively organisation, the Friends of the Settle-Carlisle Line (FoScl). Even before closure was officially announced, the Friends were campaigning against such a move. In the midst of grave talk about the future role of the viaduct came a startling declaration in the magazine Railway World for April – repeat, April – that British Railways were on the verge of completing a deal to lease the space within the arches.

The lessee, a recently-formed company called UK Reform, had been set up to operate private remand prisons under contract to the Home Office. The article was, of course, a hoax. Those who recognised it as such enjoyed this entertaining interlude in the Ribblehead story. How were the prisoners to be housed? Each arch would be infilled from ground level to the crown of the arch, giving a self-contained block. The ground floor would be the administration and security level with several floors of cells above it.

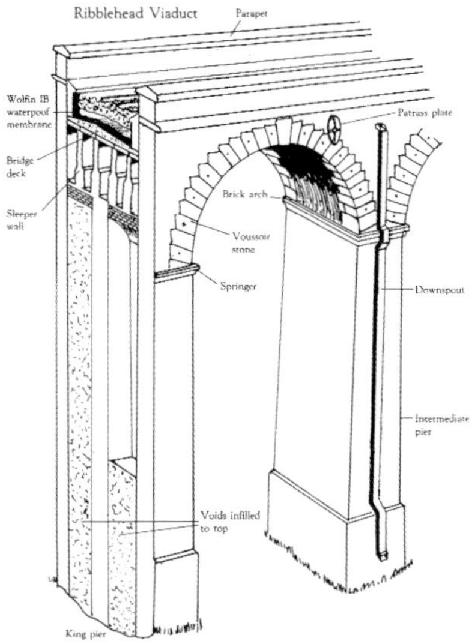

The key construction features of Ribblehead viaduct.

Because Ribblehead is a listed structure, it was not possible, as originally proposed, to clad the whole structure in a cheerful modern material such as yellow plastic panels. A compromise was reached. UK Reform would be planting Virginia creeper and honeysuckle to give the viaduct a more friendly aspect. It was pure fantasy...

At least, people were giving more than a glance at the viaduct – Bridge No 66 – prime symbol of the Settle-Carlisle line. It has had more than its fair share of maintenance because of the nature of materials used in its construction and – of considerable importance – the severity of the local climate. The construction and design of the main parts conformed with the normal standards adopted for engineering work of this type in Victorian times.

Twenty-four arches are supported on twenty-three piers and the two end abutments. The viaduct was built in four individually stable sections, each comprising six arches. Three of the piers, made considerably larger than the others, became known as King Piers. The levels of the main parts of the viaduct fall from north to south, thus sustaining the general gradient of 1 in 100.

What most visitors do not suspect is that the level of the parapet at the northern end of the viaduct is rather more than 12-ft higher than that at the southern end. Each arch has a span of 45-ft and a rise of 18-ft. The founding levels of both abutments are similar to those of the piers. Though massive, these structures are hidden in the embankment.

In addition to the limestone, which was quarried in Littledale – and also possibly, at the south side, in the vicinity of Salt Lake – gritstone for the parapet stringcourse and parapet copings came from a large quarry on Blea Moor.

Attending to a pier on Ribblehead viaduct damaged by a seepage of water, 1978.

The remorseless natural erosion caused by wind, rain, frost and thaw had led to far from subtle changes in the appearance of the viaduct. Stones were flaking and cracking. Less obvious were deficiencies in the Victorian workmanship and the stresses brought about by heavier trains. The engineers were keen to locate problems and find any cure that was necessary.

Was the degree of dilapidation – so clearly visible on the outside of the structure – symptomatic or not of more serious hidden problems? Would major repairs be required to the deck, from which water had been seeping into the arches? How much work would be needed to restore the brickwork at the interface with the masonry voussoir? Why was severe cracking occurring at the corners of many piers?

Those of us who suffered from Settle-Carlislitis were alarmed to be informed by British Rail in 1981 that Ribblehead viaduct was deteriorating to such an extent it would have to be replaced within as little as five years – or the line must be closed. At the time of the BR report, a cost of £6m for remedial work was mentioned (the estimated cost shrank on further consideration to between £2.4m and £4m).

At close quarters, the viaduct certainly looked careworn. Notices with white lettering on a red background warned all but the employees of British Rail to stay clear. A maintenance man said that during repairs on windy days, planks on the scaffolding went "up and down like piano keys." Rain, not the notorious gales, caused the major damage.

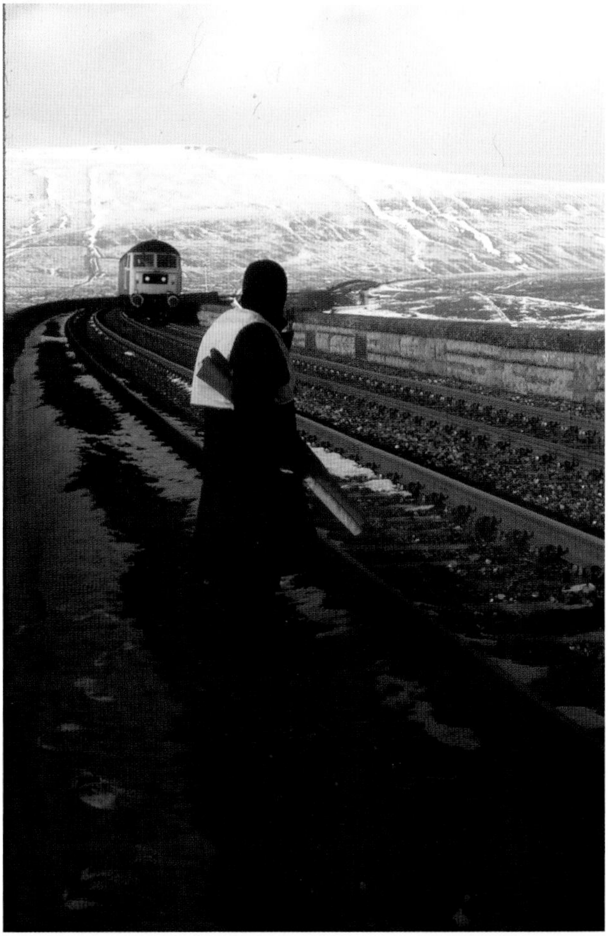

A flagman protecting a section of line under repair watches in no doubt freezing conditions as a diesel locomotive crosses the viaduct.

The various ideas put forward when the major restoration of Ribblehead viaduct was in prospect.

In April 1985 the track over the viaduct had only recently been singled. A Class 47 diesel is heading a diverted northbound express.

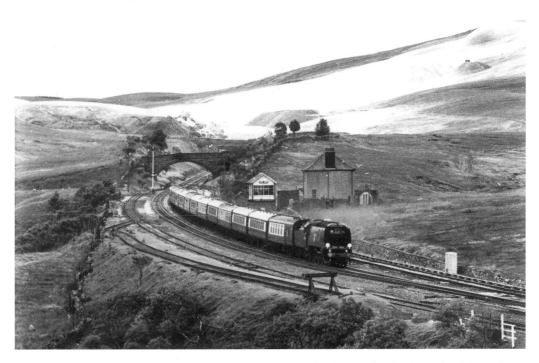

The start of the single-line section at Blea Moor, with City of Wells heading the Cumbrian Mountain Express.

Following the return of steam to the Settle-Carlisle line, ex Southern Railway Sir Lamiel forges across the viaduct on a cold winter day in 1984.

The track over the viaduct was "singled" in 1984. On a wintry day in 1978, steam returned to the Settle-Carlisle after being absent for ten years. Green Arrow appeared, speeding towards the viaduct. We would have preferred a Midland locomotive, proudly wearing its coat of "Derby red" but none was available at the time. The author's special recollection is standing, along with Mr Bannister, the last surviving member of Sir Nigel Gresley's design team, as the locomotive of this name crossed the viaduct, being little more than a smudge against the swirling vapour.

Towards the close of 1983, on a visit to Ribblehead viaduct in the company of R E Mathews, representing Alan King, the Divisional Civil Engineer, I had just heard, with some sadness, that a party of railway enthusiasts had dismantled the signal box at Aisgill – with permission – and were transporting it to a new home in an outdoor steam museum in Derbyshire. At close quarters, Ribblehead looked awesome – and careworn.

Once a week, an official from the works department arrived at Ribblehead to check on the patient's health. It was done with the aid of binoculars. Every hole and crack was clearly visible. Workmen from Penrith and Appleby would carry out any remedial work, but Ribblehead viaduct's days were numbered. "It's deteriorating faster than we can repair it," said Mr Mathews. Over £500,000 had been spent on repairs since 1970.

Some of the piers stood ankle deep in old bricks, which had long since been replaced. A number of piers had been reinforced with old and therefore rusty railway lines set vertically against the grey stones and firmly braced, giving an impression that the viaduct was wearing splints. I saw the bottom end of a Victorian downspout still in place against a pier from which other lengths had vanished. Water was now seeping through the viaduct in the wrong places. A stone from a pier-top lay half-buried in turf.

The engineers had tried to arrest the water-damage at source, by attending to the drainage high above the ground. One of the slabs of slate – actually the local type, known as Horton flag – was removed and a manhole cover fitted to enable men to explore and examine the spandrel-voids. Finding heavy iron downspouts to replace the defective spouts was not easy. The substituted material was used with varying success. Asbestos lasted for a few years. Plastic downspouting was blown from its clamps.

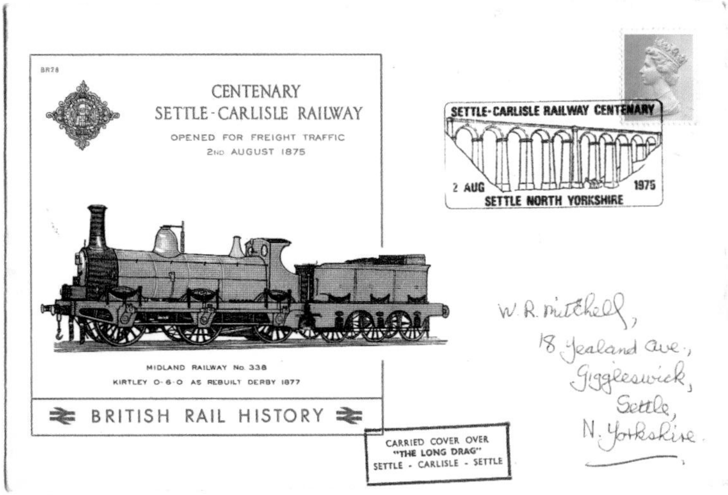

A Kirtley locomotive featured on a commemorative cover celebrating the centenary of the line being opened for freight traffic. This 0-6-0 was a mere lightweight compared with the heavy trains that have crossed Ribblehead viaduct in recent times.

A 30 mph speed restriction was in force, yet the viaduct built for Kirtley locomotives and their modest strings of carriages or wagons had been used for many years by trains weighing 900 and more tons. It had excessive use in two world wars. The Divisional Civil Engineer and his staff were aware of the stresses placed on the viaduct by wind, rain, frost and age. Yet Mr Mathews was able to say: "You have to take your hat off to the men who built Ribblehead viaduct. When you consider the primitive equipment they had, it is a fantastic piece of engineering work."

In 1983, British Rail proposed the closure of the Settle-Carlisle and Blackburn-Hellifield lines. The Transport Acts of 1962 and 1968 required the Secretary of State to take into account the hardship which would be caused by any rail closure and the wider economic and social consequences. There were many objections.

Rain, not the notorious wind, was causing the major damage to the viaduct. The average fall is about 70 inches. In 1954, over 100 inches were recorded. Five inches fell on a single day in December. Water was now seeping through in the wrong places, through cracks in slate and layers of asphalt that had deteriorated. Water found its way into the heads of the piers mixed with the fill – mortar and rubble – reducing this to a sort of clayey mud.

Water eventually trickled through the outer skin from dozens of cracks between the squared limestone, having washed away the mortar. Lime used for the original mortar was "hydraulic", brought from Barrow near Leicester. The mixture with local sand was unsatisfactory; it could now be raked out when dry and was being washed away by escaping water during the monsoons.

That "black limestone" from Littledale of which the viaduct was built is "bastard limestone". When an engineer uses the term he is not swearing but simply commenting on its nature. As noted, limestone, unlike gritstone, has no bedding grain. When compressed, it is easily shattered, either vertically or horizontally. This happens when the bedding mortar deteriorates - when one stone rests against another. The compressive force causes cracking. Pieces fall away.

In 1988, trial repairs were undertaken on king-pier No 12, intermediate pier No 13 and the associated arch. The trial was crucial in defining the nature of the problems and the means of repairing them at reasonable cost. There was no hint of turbulence to come.

Four weeks prior to the trial taking place, there was an unwelcome diversion. Batty Green was invaded by 1,000 hippies – mainly young people, who en masse had been roaming the country. The man in charge, known as Sheriff, wore a brown felt top hat of a style like that used by the Mad Hatter. By August, some 5,000 hippies were present; they slept in tents, teepees or in one of 25 buses of the clapped-out variety. And, let it be whispered, fires were lighted and some planks from the scaffolding found their way on to them.

Completed in an impressive fourteen weeks, at a cost of £380,000, the trial repairs led to an assessment of the cost of repairing the whole structure. The figure was £3 million. The assessment

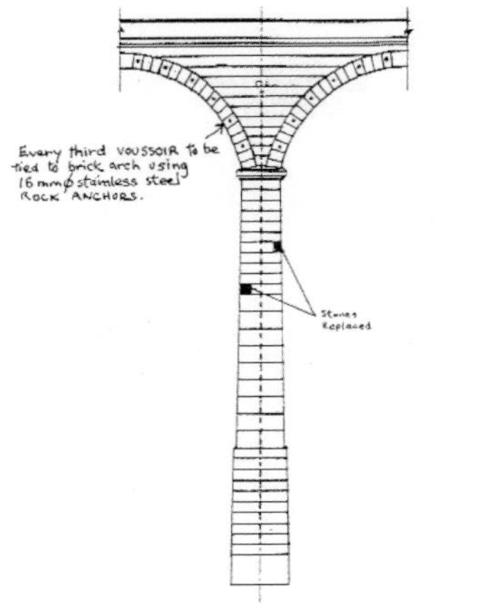

TYPICAL INTERMEDIATE PIER
(West Elevation – East Elevation similar)

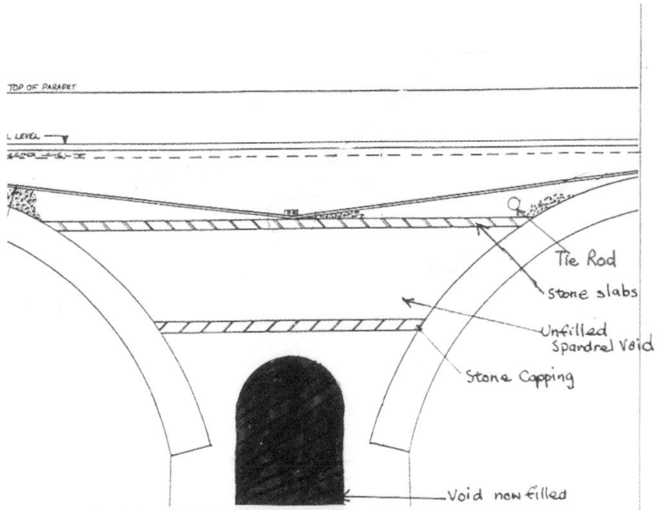

CROSS SECTION of KING PIERS 6, 12 & 18

Details relevant to the trial repairs in 1988 of king pier No 12 and intermediate pier No 13.

took place against a backdrop of governmental plans for its sale. Happily, those who built the viaduct had conformed with the drawings. Expensive major works would be unlikely.

The work took place in stormy weather. Over forty men, working over three shifts, day and night, were ceaselessly buffeted by a strong westerly wind. They gazed over moorland that was being over-run by local becks. The viaduct deck was subsequently overlaid with 2,647 square metres of a tough and durable rubberised membrane, cushioned on both top and bottom to prevent accidental puncturing by the replacement ballast or any other foreign body.

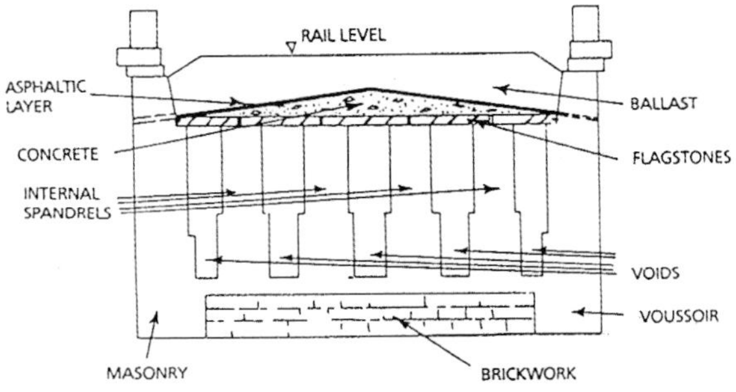

CROSS SECTION OF EXISTING DECK

Fig 1

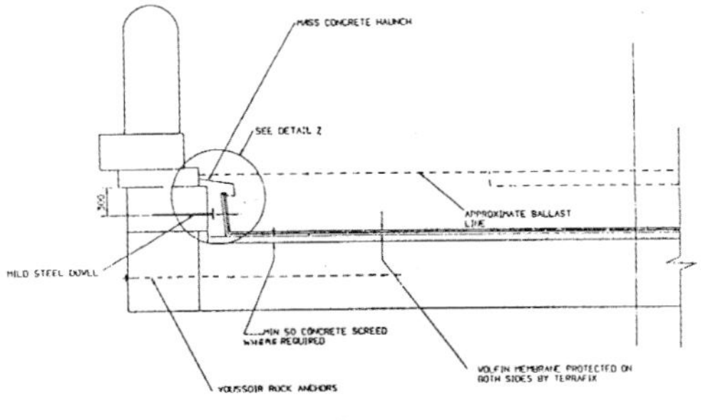

CROSS SECTION OF NEW DECK

The viaduct deck is overlaid with a durable waterproof membrane during the October 1989 repairs.

New ballast brought from Wales is laid on top of the viaduct.

In order to minimise disruption, work went on day and night. The arc lights gave an eerie glow to the normally dark and desolate moorland around Ribblehead.

Reopening on 30 October 1989 was only half an hour behind schedule!

The author has chilling memories of the Sunday on which the track was relaid. The weather was at its Pennine worst. Blustery wind and torrential rain beat against the viaduct. He sheltered behind a wagon well clear of the action. Out of the murk came the locomotive and crane, with stretches of track to be re-positioned on the newly-restored deck. After two weeks of complex operations and much hard labour, the viaduct was handed back to traffic at 06.30 hrs on Monday, October 30 – just half an hour later than had been planned.

After all this effort, would the line be closed? In a surprise announcement in Parliament, in 1989, the Government refused consent to close the line. Those who ran British Railways – like the Midland directors of Victorian days – could only shrug their shoulders and get on with the job, in this case a matter of restoration. Top of the repair list were the deteriorating viaducts and tunnel.

The saviour of the Settle-Carlisle, on 11 April, 1989, was Paul Channon, Secretary of State for Transport. He had been minded to close the line but, with a lapse of time, he had given objectors further opportunities to produce fresh evidence as to why it should be left open. Channon refused British Rail consent to close, to passenger traffic, the Settle-Carlisle line and the associated Blackburn-Hellifield line.

The trial repairs to Ribblehead Viaduct he had requested in the previous year indicated it would be much cheaper to repair the whole structure than previously thought. A new survey by the local authorities suggested that traffic on the line had continued to grow and, significantly, more people were travelling for essential purposes. "The line may continue to run at a loss, but not necessarily a large one." Mr Channon looked to all who had promised to support the line to work together "to ensure that it has a successful future and so that the case of closure will not re-emerge."

The main repair work began in July, 1990 and at its peak the labour force consisted of fifty men of various skills. It was about half the number of masons and joiners who had been associated with the viaduct when it was constructed 120 years before. The weather-gods taunted the workers with blustery winds, heavy rain and periods of hard frost.

High winds brought work to a standstill on fourteen days during the trial work in August and September, 1988. Work undertaken from scaffolding ceased when the wind speed reached 50 mph. Boards and walkway timbers were fastened down, despite which the wind was occasionally strong enough to tear boards from the upper walkways, in some cases blowing them upwards for 15-ft or more. They went over the parapet and clattered down on the tracks.

In mid-October, 1989, the track and 3,000 tonnes of ballast were removed with the aid of mechanical diggers. Of this figure, 500 tonnes were re-usable. The other material was tipped over the parapets to form a service road adequate for the passage of heavy vehicles with the equipment to pump concrete from the bottom to the bridge deck level. The special pump had a boom with a length of 140-ft. It was necessary to import 2,500 tonnes of new ballast from a quarry in North Wales.

The viaduct enmeshed in scaffolding for the 1990-91 restoration work.

Attention being given to defective brickwork under the arches.

Men working underneath the arches used some of the old methods to attend to defective brickwork. To Tony Freschini it was an uncommon privilege to stand on scaffolding at an elevation of almost 100-ft and watch two brickies at work in a way little changed in over a century. A hole was drilled to admit a T-shaped implement, one of several devised to hold an arch of metal equivalent to the arch of the viaduct. It left space for the baulks of wood to hold newly introduced brick for the two days in which the mortar would dry.

Drilling a hole for grouting on one of the piers.

Liza Pugh, a quantity surveyor, inspecting a block before carrying out precise measurements.

Piers were grouted. Cracked stones were replaced. The entire structure was re-pointed to avoid variable quality and unattractive appearance. All the repair work for which scaffolding was required had been completed by Christmas, 1991, leaving only minor works and site tidying to be completed early in 1992.

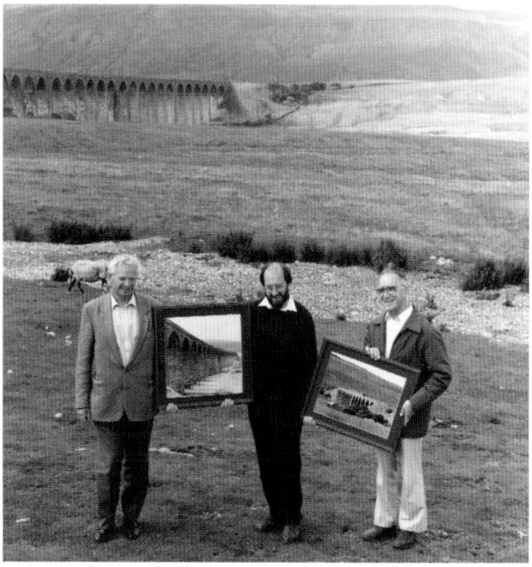

An August 1992 celebration of the completion of work on Ribblehead viaduct. From left to right are Tony Freschini (resident engineer), Geoff Bounds (project manager) and the author.

On a special plaque, within a few yards of one of the piers, a modern railway worker is depicted shaking hands with a Victorian navvy. Thus was work on Ribblehead viaduct commemorated.

Ribblehead station symbolises the smart modern state of the Settle-Carlisle line.

Arrival of an evening train bound for Leeds.

A lighter moment in the grim task of restoration was the story of a coffin which, reportedly, was propped against a parapet of the viaduct. Tony and three members of his staff had a distant view of "something". As they neared it, the object was undoubtedly a coffin, from which protruded an arm. A silver plate on the outside of the coffin was inscribed with the word "Walter". The arm was made of rubber. Grasping the lid, which was loose, Tony threw it back with a scream that made his companions flee in terror. The coffin was empty. It was, as someone remarked, 'armless.

Room for a rucksack at Ribblehead. The station is well patronised by walkers.

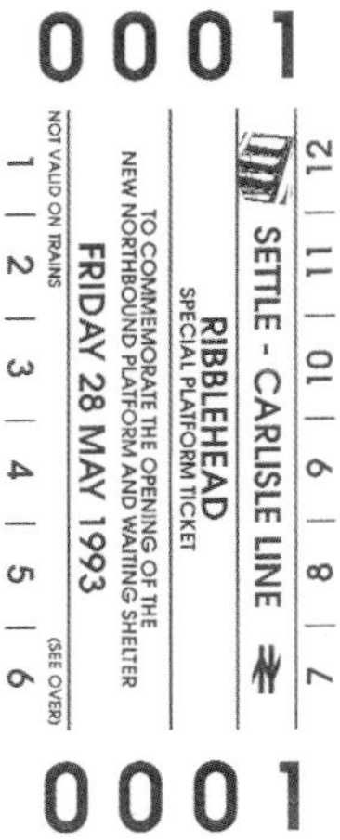

0001
12 | 11 | 10 | 9 | 8 | 7
SETTLE - CARLISLE LINE
RIBBLEHEAD
SPECIAL PLATFORM TICKET
TO COMMEMORATE THE OPENING OF THE
NEW NORTHBOUND PLATFORM AND WAITING SHELTER
FRIDAY 28 MAY 1993
NOT VALID ON TRAINS
(SEE OVER)
1 | 2 | 3 | 4 | 5 | 6
0001

Platform ticket issued when the new northbound platform was opened.

The Settle-Carlisle is the only railway line in Britain that has been designated for its entire length as a conservation area. Ribblehead viaduct has been scheduled as an Ancient Monument – a monument that is still in daily use. The bed of the old tramway, beyond Blea Moor signal box towards the Moor, has also become part of the Three Peaks footpath.

St Leonard's, formerly the chapel for "Ingleton fells", presides over what is for many people a favourite tract of Yorkshire – a silent, tucked-away area where one tends to talk in whispers. Ash trees grow from cracks between mossy blocks of limestone. Hum a few strains from Grieg and you might even see a troll. The little church presides over the last resting place of over 200 railway folk – men, women and children. Here is a poignant reminder of all those who died during the construction of the Settle-Carlisle line.

St Leonard's, Chapel-le-Dale, the last resting place of those who died at Batty Green.

The north face of Ingleborough viewed through the lych gate at St Leonard's.

To visit the church, take a brisk turn in the valley where its presence is indicated by a fingerpost. A screen of trees muffles the whine and whoosh of motor traffic. Mossy walls and trees with interlocking branches give the by-road a gloomy aspect. The rippling song of a wren has the audio effect of a pneumatic drill.

A lych-gate frames a view of St Leonard's Church and from the churchyard you can look eastwards, through a gap between trees, on to the steep northern side of Ingleborough – so steep that when John Ruskin, the Victorian philosopher, travelled up the dale on a breezy day, he marvelled that the mountain could stand without rocking. So many interments took place that the churchyard was extended, the additional land being given by Earl Bective.

A report on the consecration of additional burying ground, dated August 12, 1871, states: "On account of the terrible havoc made amongst the inhabitants at the new railway works on Blea Moor by the smallpox, the burial ground had become quite too small as the resting place of the dead. When it is stated that nearly 60 persons since last July but one have been interred in the small burial ground attached to that small but neat house of prayer, anyone who knows the place will see that the additional accommodation for the dead has not been made too soon." Over 30 persons who died in the smallpox outbreak at Batty Green lie in this burial ground.

To unite both portions of ground, the old road to the farms which lie at the foot of Whernside was broken up and a new and better road made. "All the farmers who travelled over the road to their farmstead, like sensible men, gave their willing consent to the alteration. Monday last being the day appointed for consecrating the new ground, Dr Ryan, vicar of Bradford and lately a colonial bishop, attended in place of the bishop of Ripon to perform the site of consecration."

In the early years, the clergyman was the Rev W M Harper, "a gentleman of genial spirit". He moved elsewhere in the spring of 1871 and was succeeded by the Rev E Smith; he was the incumbent when the churchyard extension was opened. The burial register presents the sad story of lives cut short by privation or disease. Plain coffins were made at a joiners' shop behind the Wheatsheaf, Ingleton, and transported to Batty Green.

Many sad tales might be told of the churchyard. On the death of a child in March, 1871, the coffin was born by men to Chapel-le-Dale. They stopped for a drink at the Hill Inn, leaving the coffin on the roadway. The "smallpox year", 1871, ended with a strange scene when the twin daughters of a miner living with his wife at Tunnel Huts, on Blea Moor, were interred. The twins had been a few days old when they died.

Notice was given to the curate, during the absence of the vicar, that the funeral would take place on 6 December. The father believed it would take place on another day, of which the curate was aware. When the funeral cortege arrived about five minutes before the time mentioned, the churchyard gates were found to be locked. No bell was being tolled. Neither the curate nor the sexton was present. The curate eventually appeared "with vexing nonchalance." He had forgotten about the funeral and had not notified the sexton. The father of the dead children borrowed tools, dug a grave, tolled the bell and then filled in the grave he had dug with his own hands.

In the churchyard, an inscribed stone near a wall, well away from the path, commemorates James Mathers, the proprietor of the Welcome Home, who died on a visit to Ingleton in "railway time". As he attempted to stop a bolting horse, James was dragged under its clattering hooves. The only other memorial in the churchyard of specific railway interest is on the right as you pass through the lych gate. Ornate, bench-type, with eroded lettering, it commemorates our old friend Job Hirst, subcontractor at Ribblehead viaduct. The Midland and fellow workmen contributed to the cost of a marble memorial fixed to a wall inside the little church.

The Settle-Carlisle was never an ordinary railway. Part of its appeal lay in the devil-may-care attitude adopted by the engineers in rough and mountainous terrain. What was intended primarily as a fast through-route to Scotland had not been humbled by the quirks of local topography. It took the straightest possible route.

If the engineers encountered a hill, they drove a tunnel through it. When a bluff was reached, a cutting was made. Every valley was exalted by having a viaduct slung across it. Several million cubic yards of material were poured into bogs that, after heavy rain, had the consistency of Yorkshire pudding mixture.

The story of the Settle-Carlisle did not end with its completion. From 1883, the locomotives operating along it were dressed in "Midland red". The line served valiantly in two world wars. It continues to serve passengers with an acceptable service. It is a major route for freight, in this case coal being transported to the power stations of South Yorkshire and Derbyshire and gypsum discharged from a siding at Kirkby Thore, which lies "over the top", in Edenvale.

For many, the highlight of their association with Ribblehead viaduct came on 22 July, 2007, when Network Rail, having a blockade between Settle Junction and Appleby for major work on the line, but being on the point of resuming normal service, extended a special dispensation to over 2,000 members of the public to cross the viaduct in what someone termed "a shingle shuffle".

Scenes during the July 2007 "shingle shuffle" over Ribblehead viaduct.

Their passage, from south to north, beginning at Ribblehead station and ending with a descent of the embankment beyond the viaduct, conformed meticulously with health and safety rules, to the extent that each person wore a conspicuously bright jacket. This joyous event had the support, and ultimately benefited the funds of the Friends of the Settle-Carlisle Line.

A tape stretched across the viaduct was formally cut by Mike Harding, after Jon Mitchell, television weatherman, had given a light-hearted forecast for the day. He said: "If it was wall-to-wall sunshine, it would not be Ribblehead weather. It's going to brighten up, though we want a breeze to keep the midges at bay. Incidentally, it's only the females that bite." He looked at the sky and said there was a thirty per cent chance of a shower.

Someone remarked that Ribblehead must be the only place on Network Rail where you might get a gale and fog at the same time. Even the weather is special.

Illustrations

Betty Harrington, courtesy of the North Craven Building Preservation Trust:
pages 47, 50, 53, 62, 74 (top).
Alan Fearnley, courtesy David Joy: 19.
Derek Cross: 100, 109.
Janet Ellerington: 14.
Peter Fox: 12, 13, 16, 32 (bottom), 40, 43, 72, 125, 145 (top + bottom), 146, 150 (top).
Roger Keech: 9.
Nigel Mussett: 32 (top)
Jack Sedgwick: 114.
R.W. Swallow: 158.
Eric Treacy: 120.
Yorkshire Post: 3, 139 (top + bottom), 151 (top), 155 (bottom left).

All other illustrations by the author or from his collection.

Also by W.R. Mitchell, available from Great Northern Books:

HANNAH HAUXWELL – 80 Years in the Dales

The Official Biography to Celebrate the 80th Birthday of this Remarkable Dales Character
Hannah captured the hearts of the nation when she was the subject of an extraordinary documentary, *Too Long a Winter*. The TV programme made her a national celebrity. Further programmes followed. She went on tours of Europe and America, shook hands with the Pope and played the piano on the Orient Express. This major book traces the extraordinary life of a delightful personality who has never lost her links with the dales countryside. It includes many previously unpublished photographs.
Fully illustrated. Hardback.

New Autumn 2009
WAINWRIGHT – Milltown to Mountain

Alfred Wainwright (1907 - 1991) became the proverbial legend in his own lifetime. He made the Lakeland fells his own through a series of hand-drawn, hand-written guide books. Over 200 fells became known as 'Wainwrights'. A society has been named ater him. His exploits have been recently emulated in the BBC television series Wainwright Walks.

This ground-breaking, richly anecdotal and personal book about Wainwright also recalls his young days in the Lancashire milltown of Blackburn and his fascination – as a lone walker – for wild places in Lancashire, along the Pennines, which have been described as 'the backbone of England', and in the north-west extremities of Scotland. He devised the popular Coast to Coast Walk, from the Irish Sea at St Bees to the North Sea at Robin Hood's Bay.

The author, Bill Mitchell, is one of a quartet of fell walkers who were personal friends of AW and his wife Betty. She also features in this book, which – far from being a dull treatise on fell walking – enters the quirky, ever fascinating world of its best-known exponent and the wife who played a strong supporting role.
Fully illustrated. Hardback.